CW01261224

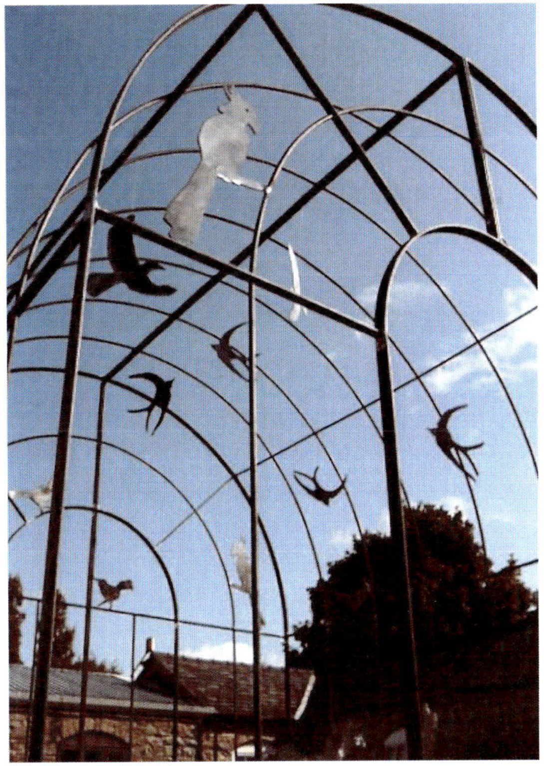

'Two Circles in a Stone Bridge', Tout Quarry, Portland Bill, Dorset, 1983. Designer: Paul Cooper.

CONCEPTUALIST LANDSCAPES

An alternative way to design gardens

Paul Cooper

PACKARD PUBLISHING LIMITED
CHICHESTER

CONCEPTUALIST LANDSCAPES

An alternative way to design gardens

© 2014 Paul Cooper

First published in 2014 by Packard Publishing Limited, Forum House, Stirling Road, Chichester, West Sussex, PO19 7DN, United Kingdom.

The Author asserts his rights as the originator of the text and designated designs. No part of this publication may be reproduced, stored in a retrieval system, transmitted in any form, electronic, mechanical, photocopying, recording or otherwise without either the written permission of the Publisher or a licence allowing restricted copying issued by the Copyright Licensing Agency, or its international equivalents. This book may not be lent, resold, hired out or otherwise disposed of by way of trade in any form other than that in which it was originally published without the prior permission of the Publisher.

The front-cover, half-title, title and contents-page photographs of his designs were taken by the Author.

ISBN 978 185341 145 8

Commissioned, edited and prepared for press by Michael Packard.

Designed and laid out by HiLite Design and Reprographics Limited, Marchwood, Southampton, Hampshire.

Printed and bound in the United Kingdom by PublishPoint, KnowledgePoint Limited, Winnersh, Wokingham, Berkshire.

Acknowledgements

The majority of the photographs were taken by the Author, Paul Cooper. Others are gratefully acknowledged and with many thanks:

Acres Wild	5
Julia Barton	11
BCA Landscape	17
Patrick Blanc	45
Cao | Perrot	23
Delaney & Chin	5, 16, 40
Tony Heywood	12, 33
Jean-Claude Hurni	90-92
Patricia Johanson	21
Lutsko Associates - Landscape	12
Marianne Majerus	18, 28, 32, 51, 54-55, 56-57, 64-65, 78-79, 80-81, 86, 88
Teru Mitani	44
Jereon Musch/West 8 Urban Design & Landscape Architecture	35
Martha Schwartz/MSP Ltd	27, 30
National Gallery of Victoria	1
Plant Architect Inc.	24
Jean-François Vézina/Claude Cormier & Associés	10, 31
Wagner Hodgson Landscape Architecture	25

List of Artists, Galleries & Design Practices

Acres Wild (Debbie Roberts & Ian Smith), 1 Helm Cottages, Nuthurst, West Sussex, RH13 6RG, UK.

Julia Barton, Briar Cottage, Donkleywood, Hexham, Northumberland, NE48 1AH, UK.

BCA Landscape, 19 Old Hall Street, Liverpool, L3 9JQ, UK; Studio I, Rochelle School, Arnold Circus, Shoreditch, London, E2 7ES, UK.

Cao | Perrot, 3511 West 6th Street, Studio 5, Los Angeles, CA 90020, USA; 20 Mail François Mitterand, 35000 Rennes, Brétagne, France.

Paul Cooper, Ty Bryn, Old Radnor, Presteigne, Powys, Wales, LD8 2RN, UK.

Claude Cormier & Associés Inc., 1223 des Carrières, Studio A, Montréal, QC, Canada H2S 2B1.

Delaney & Chin, 600 Illinois Street, San Francisco, CA 94107, USA.

Tony Heywood, 39 Bathurst Mews, London, W2 2SB, UK.

Patricia Johanson, 179 Nickmush Road, Buskirk, New York 12028, USA.

Lutsko Associates - Landscape, 2815 18th Street, San Francisco, CA 94110, USA.

Teru Mitani, Chiba University, Graduate School of Horticulture, Department of Landscape Design, 648 Matsudo, Matsudo-shi, Chiba-ken, 271-8510, Japan.

National Gallery of Victoria, 180 St Kilda Road, Melbourne, VIC 3004, Australia.

PLANT Architect Inc., 101 Spadina Avenue, Suite 208, Toronto, ON, Canada M5V 2K2.

Martha Schwartz Partners Ltd, 65-69 East Road, London, N1 6AH, UK.

www.verticalgardenpatrickblanc.com

Wagner Hodgson Landscape Architecture, 7 Marble Avenue, Burlington, VT 05401, USA.

West 8 Urban Design & Landscape Architecture b.v., Schiehaven 13M, 3024 EC Rotterdam, The Netherlands.

CONTENTS

Preface	vii
1 INTRODUCING THE IDEA	1
2 THE THEORY	4
What is Conceptualist Design?	4
The Influence of Art	6
Land and Environmental Art	6
The Garden as Art	8
3 IN PRACTICE	9
The Hard Landscape	9
The Soft Landscape	10
Conceptualist Planting	11
4 THE DESIGN PROCESS	13
The Design Brief	13
Deciding on a Strategy	13
Getting Inspiration – Gathering Source Material	14
Site-based (Strategy 1)	15
Present-day or Proposed Activity (Strategy 2)	15
Historical Reference (Strategy 3)	16
Site and Social History	16
Client History (Strategy 4)	17
Project-specific – Single Visual Motif (Strategy 5)	18
Imported Visual Motifs (Strategy 6)	19
Eclectic	20
Personal	21
Alternative Ways of Making (Strategy 7)	22
Autobiographical (Strategy 8)	22
Developing the Idea	24
Working with the Site	24
The Narrative Approach	26
The Visual Method	29
Autobiographical & Art-based	33
Ways of Making (Building ideas)	34
Unconventional from the Commonplace	34
Paving to Create an Illusion	36
Drawing with Bricks	36
Painting in Concrete and Turf	36
Constructivist Timbers	37
Modern Materials and Methods	37
Portable and Disposable	38
Theatrical and Kinetic	41
Planting Technologies	45
5 SELECTED PROJECTS	47
Site-specific	47
Two Circles in a Stone Bridge	48
Grizedale Forest Sculpture Trail	50
Roof Garden – Chelsea Mews Property	51
Garden at 'Torrens'	52
Garden Room – Leonard Hotel, London	54
Narrative-based	56
Allegorical Garden	56
Greening of Industry	58
Boy's Own Garden	60
Football Fantasy	62
A Biographical Odyssey	64
Ocean to a Garden	66
New Ways of Making	68
Hanging Garden of Chelsea	68
Instant Garden	70
Floating Garden	73
Just What Is It?	74
Cool and Sexy Garden	76
Multi-Media Garden	78
Night Garden	80
Garden as Art	82
Ford 'Carden'	82
Heavy Metal Garden	84
Rothko Garden	86
Prism Garden	87
Climate Cases	88
Eden Laboratory	90
Specialist	93
Square-Dance Garden	93
Sensory Garden	94
Further Reading	102
Index	102

LIST OF ILLUSTRATIONS

'Two Circles in a Stone Bridge', Dorset, Paul Cooper	ii
'Underground Garden', London, Paul Cooper	viii
'Landscape of the Summer Solstice', Paul Nash	1
'Equinox Garden', Paul Cooper	2-3
Private house, Surrey, Acres Wild	4-5
Private residence, San Francisco, Topher Delaney	5
'A Landscape for Measuring Distance and Time', Paul Cooper	7
Place d'Youville, Montréal, Claude Cormier et Associés	10
'Resurrection', Chatham County Jail, Savannah, Julia Barton	11
Ranch, south of San Francisco, Ron Lutsko	12
Courtyard, University of San Francisco, Topher Delaney	16
'Face of Liverpool', Andy Thomson, BCA Landscape	17
'A Biographical Odyssey', Paul Cooper	18
Hodgkinson Centre, Acute Psychiatric Unit, Lincoln County Hospital, Paul Cooper	19
'Pop Goes the Garden', New Eden Magazine/Paul Cooper	20
'Endangered Garden' and 'Ribbon Worm', Patricia Johanson	21
'The Calling', Kinsale, Tony Heywood	22
'Glass Garden', Andy Cao	23
'Sweet Farm', Québec, Plant Architect Inc.	24
'Hilltop Residence', Vermont, Keith Wagner	25
'Splice Garden', Cambridge, MA, Martha Schwartz	27
'Allegorical Garden', Kilcot, Gloucestershire, Paul Cooper	28
'The Citadel', Commerce, CA, Martha Schwartz	30
'Lipstick Forest', Montréal, Claude Cormier & Associés	31
'Night Garden', London, Paul Cooper	32
'The Echo'. Belfast Botanic Garden, Tony Heywood	33
'Interpolis' Garden, Tilburg, West 8	35
'Torrens', Weybridge, Paul Cooper	36
'Instant Garden', BBC TV, Paul Cooper & Cliff Gorman	38
'Just What Is It? Hampton Court Flower Show, Paul Cooper	39
'Blue Garden', San Francisco, Topher Delaney	40
'Multi-media Garden', London, Paul Cooper	41
YKK Research & Development Centre, Tokyo, Toru Mitani	44
The 'Living Wall', Athenaeum Hotel, London, Patrick Blanc	45
'The Heavy Metal Garden', Gloucestershire, Paul Cooper	46
'Two Circles in a Stone Bridge', Portland, Dorset, Paul Cooper	48-49
Grizedale Forest Sculpture Trail proposal, Paul Cooper	50
A Roof Garden, Chelsea Mews, London, Paul Cooper	51
Garden at 'Torrens', 1930s-style property, Weybridge, Paul Cooper	52-53
A Garden Room, Leonard Hotel, London, Paul Cooper	54-55
'An Allegorical Garden', Kilcot, Gloucestershire, Paul Cooper	56-57
'The Greening of Industry', Chelsea Flower Show 1990, Paul Cooper	58-59
'A Boy's Own Garden', Chelsea Flower Show 1998, Paul Cooper	60-61
'A Football Fantasy', Battersea, London, Paul Cooper	62-63
'A Biographical Odyssey', Muswell Hill, London, Paul Cooper	64-65
'Ocean to Garden', Chelsea Flower Show 2008, Paul Cooper	66-67
'The Hanging Garden of Chelsea', Chelsea Flower Show, 1991, Paul Cooper	68-69
'The Instant Garden', BBC TV 'Gardens by Design' 1989, Paul Cooper & Cliff Gorman	70-72
'The Floating Garden', Chelsea Flower Show, Paul Cooper	73
'Just What Is It?' Hampton Court Flower Show 1989, Paul Cooper	74-75
'Cool and Sexy Garden', Chelsea Flower Show, 1994, Paul Cooper	76-77
'Multi-Media Garden', Golders Green, London, Paul Cooper	78-79
'The Night Garden', London, Paul Cooper	80-81
'The Ford 'Carden'', BBC Gardener's World Live Show 1995, Birmingham, Paul Cooper	82-83
'The Heavy Metal Garden', Gloucestershire, Paul Cooper	84-85
'The Rothko Garden' London, Paul Cooper	86
'The Prism Garden', London, Paul Cooper	87
'The Climate Cases', Chelsea Flower Show 2003, Paul Cooper	88-89
'The Eden Laboratory' experimental garden, Métis International Garden Festival 2002, Paul Cooper	90-92
'The Square Dance Garden', Lincoln County Hospital Psychiatric Unit, Paul Cooper	93
'The Sensory Garden', Newbus Grange, Darlington	94-101

PREFACE

The use of the word 'conceptualist' to describe a landscape or a garden might be considered new, but the design methodology that is associated with the term has been practised for at least a quarter of a century. Only recently has it been identified and recognized as a distinct motif of garden design.

It is thanks in the most part to the writer and critic Tim Richardson that this form of landscape and garden design now has a name. When attempting to find a shorthand way to describe a seemingly diverse body of work, which included gardens by the likes of Martha Schwartz, Topher Delaney and Claude Cormier, Richardson realized that they all had a common denominator. The design of each landscape or garden was based on an 'Idea' or concept.

When one examines the work of the designers highlighted by Richardson, one is not only struck by the sheer variety of design but how original and imaginative it is. Many of the gardens and landscapes invite the sort of critical evaluation normally reserved for the world of contemporary art

It has to be admitted that some conceptualist creations do belong more to the world of art than that of gardening, but certainly not all. One of the aims of this book is to demonstrate that conceptualism is not a fringe activity for the few, or a recipe for outrageous and impractical creations, but a design philosophy that is making a major contribution to mainstream garden and landscape design. It is a worthwhile ambition, both in terms of expanding the definition of garden design, and in the encouragement it gives to those who believe in designing with imagination and meaning in whatever context.

First, I must make it clear that this book is not an instruction manual on how to design a conceptualist garden. Conceptualist design is not a singular style with a visual language that can be assimilated or imitated: it simply does not lend itself to such an approach. One conceptualist garden is likely to look very different to another, but all are idea-driven and the work of designers with inquisitive and enquiring minds.

Most important, the book should not be regarded as a convenient and easy source of design ideas or a shop window for 'off-the-peg' solutions. The gardens described and illustrated are bespoke designs for unique commissions. Gaining some understanding of how the designer, architect or artist arrived at his or her personal solution is what matters. As with solving a mathematical problem, to simply crib the answer is both dishonest and pointless.

The book sets out to provide an insight into the design process associated with conceptualism. To de-mystify what is often considered to be shrouded in 'art-speak', and to make accessible a different but no less pragmatic way of designing gardens and landscapes, releases the imagination and facilitates decision-making. It reveals that for the most part the conceptualist way is neither intimidating theory, nor a wholesale rejection of more conventional design principles as some might suggest.

So, I begin with an explanation of what is meant by conceptualist landscape design and the philosophy that links all its practitioners. Its undeniable relationship with 'Conceptual Art' and 'Pop Art' is also examined.

The majority of the text is devoted to an in-depth review of the design process and associated methodologies that are synonymous with conceptualist garden design; a process that begins with a search for an IDEA, or related ideas, which will determine all aspects of the design of the landscape or garden.

A portfolio of case studies also amplifies the rest of the text. Learning by example will undoubtedly help the reader to understand a way of designing that, although bound by a common philosophy, is varied in both its adopted methods and outcomes. The studies demonstrate that the conceptualist approach can provide inspirational solutions for all forms of gardens and landscapes, from modest backyards to challenging public spaces.

As an acknowledged practitioner of this type of garden design I have been asked to refer to examples of my own work, mainly because a first-hand account of my own modest efforts — successful or otherwise — is inevitably more accurate and perceptive than the most thoroughly researched projects by other designers.

There are many garden professionals who claim that the 'conceptualist approach' is irrelevant and inappropriate to the design of domestic gardens, and that it belongs to the 'Art for Art's Sake' or 'Garden for Garden's Sake', avant-garde world of events and festivals. Furthermore when commissioned, usually for the public or commercial sector, the results rarely fall within the accepted definition of a garden, particularly when it comes to plants and planting.

There is, currently, an interest in what is known as conceptual design. In a garden this is intended to convey an idea or theme or symbolism to the onlooker and need not involve the creation of a 'traditional' garden. It is a form of art in the landscape in which the concept may have an importance beyond practical considerations and where the boundaries between pure and applied art may be breached … Private clients, however, rarely want to live with this type of project.

(Extract from B. Hunt & E. Whateley, *Creative Connections — Aspects of the Garden Design Process*, Packard Publishing, Chichester.)

This book sets out to prove that statement to be not entirely accurate by showing that conceptualist garden design can provide both a stimulating and practical solution whatever the challenge. Not only does it respect horticulture but it is instrumental in encouraging new ways of using plants.

Finally, I use the word 'conceptualist' rather than 'conceptual' for a reason: it helps to distinguish garden design 'conceptualism' from that of art. With regard to the latter 'conceptual' means just that; a form of art that seeks to minimize physical expression and to reduce the reliance on artefacts. This is certainly not the case with conceptualist garden design.

I also try to avoid the use of 'theme'. In art and design it is defined as 'a unifying idea or motif developed throughout a work'. In garden design it is often used in a more generic way, especially at flower shows, where titles such as 'Romantic Woodland Garden', 'Seaside Garden' and 'Cottage Garden' prevail. And a 'theme' is often loosely applied, whereas in conceptualist garden design the 'idea' has a much stronger, all-embracing influence.

Paul Cooper

An underground garden, London.
Designer: Paul Cooper.
Photo: Paul Cooper

This conceptualist design for an op-art garden was designed for an underground house in London in 2011. The walls of the sunken courtyard were clad in vertical slats at regular and variable intervals. The white slats also created interference patterns and faint colour effects. The space functioned as both patio and water garden with plants in isolated and separately managed containers. The fountains could be switched off when an outdoor sitting area was required. The water collection tank beneath the paving also acted as an emergency reservoir to prevent the property from flooding.

1 INTRODUCING THE 'IDEA'

All good garden design involves ideas and imagination. How that creativity is directed determines the type of garden that will be produced. Usually, there is an all-embracing design concept which most often relates to a distinct style of design philosophy.

In Modernist and Minimalist design, this involves a rejection of frivolous decoration in favour of a reductionist approach which puts the emphasis on form following function: a style characterized by straight lines, plain walls and single-species planting (see *The Minimalist Garden* by Christopher Bradley-Hole, Mitchell-Beazley, London).

In contrast, designers such as Julie Toll prefer a different sensibility, one that evokes an earlier age, which is intrinsically very English and, although not shy of the formal, frequently includes grass meadows and informal planting to connect the designer-made landscape with nature.

All landscape or garden architects face numerous design decisions. They may opt for an overall approach that is geometric or organic, formal or informal, and so on. But the peculiarities of the site and preferences of the client will inevitably ask questions of designers as they stare at the blank sheet of paper or computer screen in front of them.

It is at this point that imagination is required. In conventional design, this will usually manifest itself in the development of a series of connected ideas, concerning such issues as the lawn, paving, planting and the shape or form of these elements. These decisions are directed or guided by a preferred design philosophy; and sometimes aided by design manuals which outline the principles — proportion and balance, movement and direction, or colour and tone — that the authors regard as essential to 'good' and aesthetically pleasing design.

In conceptualist design it is a SINGLE IDEA or closely-related ideas which, from the very start of the creative process, guide the hand of the designer.

Paul Nash (1889–1946), 'Landscape of the Summer Solstice', © Tate, London, 2014, courtesy the National Gallery of Victoria, Melbourne, Australia.

To put this in context: when I was first persuaded to try my hand at designing gardens, the only relevant experience I had was from working as an artist. My planting knowledge was zero and, although I did have a colleague who could provide horticultural expertise, I was still faced with the problem of where to start. I had to devise an alternative way of designing a garden. Unknowingly, I adopted a conceptualist approach, as this very early, tentative effort shows. (The photos were taken soon after it was completed.)

The Equinox Garden. Designer: Paul Cooper.

1–2	Specimen shrub with gold foliage, e.g., *Choisya ternata* 'Sundance', *Philadelphus coronarius* 'Aureus'.		*Ceanothus* vars plus ground cover, e.g., *Vinca minor*.
3–8	Lower-growing golden plants, e.g., *Phormium tenax* 'Variegatum'. *Juniperus pfitzerana* 'Aurea'.	64–68	Climbers with dark foliage and flowers, e.g., *Hydrangea petiolaris*.
		34–40 and 42	Rich, dense, green foliage, e.g., *Elaeagnus × ebbingei*, *Lonicera pileata*.
9–13	Variegated shrubs, e.g., *Euonymus fortunei* 'Emerald and Gold', *Lonicera nitida* 'Baggesen's Gold'.	41	Silver 'halo' for pool, e.g., *Stachys lanata*.
		43	Small specimen tree, e.g., *Pyrus salicifolia* 'Pendula'.
14–22	Shrubs with blue/mauve foliage and flowers, e.g., *Caryopteris × clandonensis* 'Heavenly Blue', rosemary, *Ceanothus* vars, *Hebe* 'Autumn Glory'.	47	Heathers with bronze and golden foliage, e.g., *Calluna* 'Blazeaway', *Erica* 'Foxhollow'.
		48–60	Mixed shrubs in 'warm' shades for year-round effect, e.g., *Cornus* 'Westonbirt', *Spiraea* 'Goldmound', *Mahonia* 'Charity', *Cotinus coggyria* 'Royal Purple'.
23–26	Ground cover in gravel in purples and blues, e.g., *Ajuga reptans* 'Atropurpurea', creeping thyme.		
27 and 44–46	Upright conifers in four sizes, e.g., *Chamaecyparis lawsonia* 'Elwoodii'.	61–63	Climbers on trellis in shades of yellow and orange, e.g., *Jasminum nudiflorum*, climbing roses 'Albertine', 'Golden Showers'.
28, 29	Dense, dark foliage, e.g., *Viburnum tinus* with underplanting, e.g., *Vinca minor*.		
30–33	Dark-foliage wall shrubs, e.g., *Pittosporum*,	69–71	Darker, twining climbers, e.g., *Vitis coignetiae*.

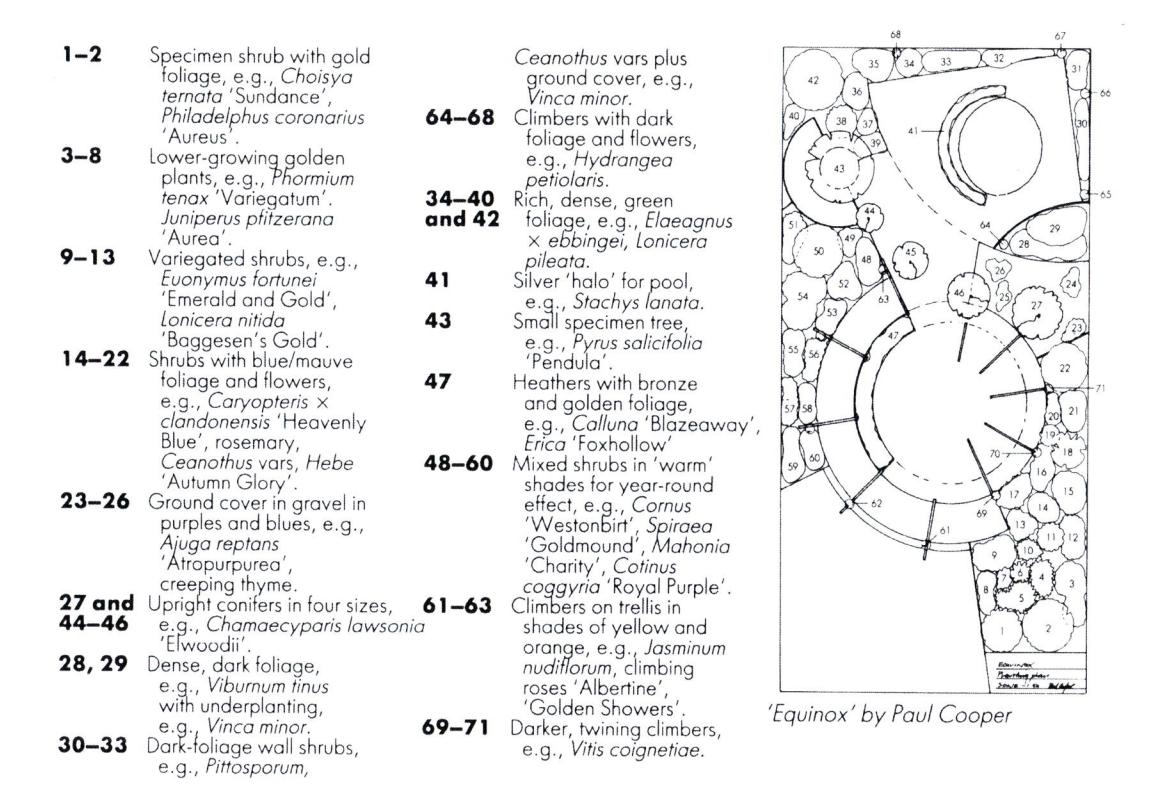

'Equinox' by Paul Cooper

This domestic garden was inspired by a description of Paul Nash's painting on the previous page 1. It is entitled 'The Landscape of the Summer Solstice' and presents the fact of equal day and night. Nash in his catalogue notes added:

Again the thought of division into light and darkness in equal parts suggests a divided space wherein a landscape on one side is lit by the setting sun, while the other lies under the influence of a rising moon. This in turn determines certain dominant colours: red and deep yellow, with a range of fading and dying rose and pink, and blue from its palest cold tints, deepening to tones of the night.

That concise statement was the IDEA. It was all I needed and determined every aspect of the design. The image of the sun and the moon gave me the prominent features of the garden, which was divided diagonally into two distinct areas defined by tone and colour.

THE EQUINOX GARDEN

2 THE THEORY

'A landscape can be about anything.'
Martha Schwartz

What is Conceptualist Garden Design?

As mentioned in the Preface, Tim Richardson originally coined the term 'Conceptualist Landscape Design' in the mid-1990s. He used it to define and categorize the work of a group of designers whose work was characterized by its narrative wit, use of artificial materials and bold colour.

Their work was the antithesis of Modernism, with its rational adherence to form following function, and the reductionism of gardens inspired by 1960s Minimalism. Yet neither did it adhere to the 'decoration for decoration sake' of the Romantic tradition, nor had it blindly adopted the eclectic tendencies of Post-Modernism. Also, it was clearly at odds with the resurgence of naturalistic and wildflower gardening.

What Richardson discovered, or perceived as distinct and new, was the use of an idea or related ideas as starting points for a landscape or garden design. The all-embracing central 'IDEA' (or motif) was the principal driving force in the design process from drawing to physical realization.

Richardson concedes that much garden design could be regarded as 'conceptualist', and it is true to say that many of the gardens and landscapes created over the centuries have been an expression of a single notion. Richardson cites Japanese Zen Gardens as an obvious example, and also those of Lutyens and Jekyll. With regards to the latter, an all-embracing vision of life and style – formulated by the Arts and Crafts movement – underpins the design and every detail related to it.

One could also add John Brookes's concept of the 'outdoor room' to the list, and the 'less is more' philosophy of Mies van der Rohe, which was adopted by the minimalist school of garden design. But in both cases the 'concept' is essentially a directive or instruction. In conceptualist design the IDEA IS THE GARDEN.

The difference between a garden created using conventional design methods and one which is conceptualist can be seen below.

The landscape architects Debbie Roberts and Ian Smith of 'Acres Wild' have produced some of Britain's most beautiful contemporary gardens in a style that marries architectural structure with a more natural-looking informality in what can be best described as 'picturesque' in manner. Their large gardens are essentially a series of gardens within a garden; a formal garden, herb garden, rock garden, pools and water features, and so on, all linked by paths and lawns. The design of each element is distinctive, but all take inspiration from the world of gardens and gardening. Their designs are a composite of a number of garden-based ideas.

*Private Residence, San Francisco, California.
Designer: Topher Delaney.*

*Private house and garden, Surrey.
Designers: Debbie Roberts & Ian Smith, Acres Wild.*

The American landscape architect Topher Delaney employs a very different approach for a private residence in San Francisco. Similar to the Acres Wild garden, it is a series of connected spaces, but here they are part of a single, continuous idea that meanders through the landscape. Delaney chooses a palette of materials — steel, granite setts, river pebbles, large stones, concrete and grass — which she uses throughout the garden. The courtyards and similar spaces are linked visually by the materials, which are shaped and formed into curves and circles that respond to the undulating terrain of the site.

The Influence of Art

It is difficult to discuss conceptualist garden and landscape design without reference to its relationship with contemporary art. We have to look back almost a century to discover the origins of the art that was to influence conceptualist designers.

In 1913, when the Swiss artist Marcel Duchamp exhibited a bicycle wheel fixed horizontally on a kitchen stool, he also turned the world of art upside down. The 'work' had required minimal intervention by the 'artist'. It was essentially a 'found object' with a stool as a pedestal placed in an art gallery.

With this simple act he had challenged the relevance of aesthetics in art. He had chosen the wheel because it was commonplace, not because it looked beautiful. By jettisoning values such as craftsmanship and the uniqueness of the art object, he had also re-written the prevailing definition of sculpture.

Marcel Duchamp was a leading member of the Dadaists, a group of nihilistic artists and intellectuals, who engaged in questioning the very nature of art. Yet what seemed at first counter-productive did not make sculptors redundant, instead it served to liberate their art from traditional conventions and preconceptions. The 'ready-made' bicycle wheel is 'art as idea'. In other words anything has the potential to be art, with all the freedom this implies. And it is this philosophy, transferred to the garden that underpins conceptualist landscape design. 'A Landscape CAN be about anything.'

Many conceptualist gardens are aesthetically challenging. Seeking to make beautiful gardens is not a primary concern. This does not mean that the gardens and landscapes are not pleasing to the eye, only that such a subjective value is as a consequence of the design process rather than an objective.

In the 1960s 'Dada' was to be influential in the emergence of 'Assemblage Art' and 'Pop Art'. Pop, with its frequent use of the kitsch and the commonplace, represented an effort by a new generation of artists keen to release art from elitist or highbrow values. Pop was never a recognizable international 'style'. Instead it manifested itself in many different guises with artists finding their own, individual way of responding to Pop culture.

Pop's youthful irreverence and inherent individualism is at the heart of conceptualist garden design. And Pop's imagery, visual brashness or simple playfulness is plainly visible in many conceptualist landscapes.

Land and Environmental Art

In the 1970s, Dadaism re-emerged as 'Conceptual Art' and 'Land Art', both of which seemed to challenge art's value as a commodity. Conceptual art did its best to shun any form of visual representation. Land Art took artists away from the studio, the gallery and the city. Sculptors such as Robert Smithson and Michael Heizer sought the remoteness of the American Mid-West to create works that were made with the material of, and in, the landscape. The way these artists considered the land, both physically and intellectually, has certainly influenced landscape design, and is particularly visible in the work of Janis Hall and Charles Jencks (see Further Reading, p. 102).

Conceptualist landscape and garden design, however, is not the same as Conceptual Art, Land Art or Dadaism, principally because garden design inevitably involves an element of function. 'In all cases function in the broadest sense must coexist with concept and distinguishes conceptual gardens from conceptual art' (Richardson). But in its radical tendencies, the desire to challenge tradition and preconceptions, and to flirt with controversy, the garden design equivalent maintains a link with its artistic spiritual home.

*'A Landscape for Measuring Distance and Time',
Ambleside, Cumbria.
Designer: Paul Cooper.*

The idea for this site-specific work for the 'Exposed to the Elements' land art and garden show in Cumbria took as its starting point the mountainous topography of the location. It suggested a solution that would connect with both the surrounding landscape and the sky above. The overall layout was based on the contours of the site. Components of the work could be viewed collectively to form alignments with distant man-made and natural features. The geometry of the sculptural elements enabled both the measurement of terrestrial distances and real time. The meaning of the existing grassy mound was transformed not by reshaping the earth but by the addition of imported stones in a manner similar to ancient sites such as Stonehenge.

LAND AND ENVIRONMENTAL ART 7

Like Pop Art, conceptualist gardens and landscapes do not conform to a recognizable single style. No manifesto of common intent or direction exists. Some gardens are idiosyncratic and distinctly personal in their content, but they all represent a realization of an idea, which has determined the design and bears the designer's signature. Conceptualist garden design is about a new 'way of working' that involves meaningful rather than arbitrary decision-making. It is this that connects all the designers referred to in this book.

Although there is no consistent visual identity, there are certain characteristics that are common to many conceptual gardens. A 'readable' narrative may be discernible in the landscape design. There is often humour and satire. In contrast to the 'monochrome of modernism', an enthusiasm for vibrant colour and an eagerness to employ new or unconventional materials and methods is evident.

In many ways conceptualist garden design is simply the acceptance of the principle that like modern art, contemporary garden design can also be 'about anything'. As a consequence, the definition of a garden has been radically expanded and new ways of creating gardens have been introduced.

The Garden as Art

The garden festivals of recent years have seen a blurring of the boundary between art and garden design. Detached from both function and a building, they have allowed the creators of these gardens a greater freedom of expression than is usual within the discipline. Festival and show gardens have played a significant part in the redefining of garden and landscape design. They have provided an opportunity for unhindered experimentation both in concept and execution.

As far as garden design is concerned, the garden festivals provide the opportunity to bring new ideas into the public domain. I once made an analogy with the Paris Fashion Shows. The avant-garde gardens are like cat-walk clothing, outrageous and usually impractical, but nevertheless bursting with imaginative ideas that will eventually filter down to the high street.

The freedom of artistic expression enjoyed at the festivals has certainly attracted conceptualist designers. But they have also provided an opportunity for visual artists to consider the garden itself as a means of expression, in the same way as 'performance' artists had previously adopted the theatre. As a result it is inevitable that some of the creations are more art than garden.

At Chaumont in France the imposition of an occasional horticultural theme has helped to keep the focus on the garden, while at Métis in Canada the lack of one has led to the creation of more ambiguous works. I voiced my opinion on festival gardens in 2007:

The garden shows and festivals take the idea of the garden away from its traditional context; its role within domestic or public environment is marginalized. Free of the restraints of situation or client requirements it is easy for garden design to enter into the domain of environmental or installation art. The same would happen to architecture if its basic function as a shelter were discarded. An abstract configuration of walls is not architecture.

There comes a point where the use of the word 'garden' in the context of a festival becomes obsolete. In my opinion, many of the creations of the festivals are first and foremost ART. They extend the parameters of ART, rather than the definition of a GARDEN. At best the festivals are a melting pot for ideas, which can be introduced into the vocabulary of garden design.

There is another issue. The use of plant material often appears as an afterthought or as a means to justify the work as a 'garden' — a gesture to help assure one that it IS a garden and not an art installation. Conversely it also serves to indicate that plants ARE important to the art of the garden.

3 IN PRACTICE

Garden design is unique in that it usually involves the combination of the vegetable and mineral: living (plants), natural materials (stone or wood) and the synthetic (concrete, plastic etc.). While it is true to say that the design of a conceptualist garden is unlikely to have been determined by recourse to garden design's traditional points of reference, such as horticulture and architecture, these are not discarded.

Conceptualist design does not represent a wholesale rejection of conventional garden or landscape design. Neither does it ignore basic design theory and practice.

An art school foundation course provided me with an awareness of the potential of line, texture, colour, and an understanding of space and three-dimensional form. (NB: Many of these topics in relation to garden design are dealt with in the companion Workshop publication *Creative Connections — Aspects of the Garden Design Process* by Barbara Hunt and Elizabeth Whateley).

The significant difference is that in conceptualist design these principles are applied as a means to an end rather than the end in itself and sometimes 'rules' are intentionally broken.

Conceptualist design is no different to any other genre of landscape design because it too must expect to fulfil a function or provide a service. It will likely have to satisfy predetermined objectives and may also have to resolve inherited problems, such as those associated with the site: sloping, heavily shaded, poor soil or no soil and so on.

What conceptualist garden design does reject, and aims to avoid, is making aesthetic decisions that could be regarded as arbitrary. Although most of its practitioners would concede that it is impossible to jettison all subjective or intuitive creativity.

The Hard Landscape

Practical and safety considerations are just as important in a conceptual garden as in a conventional one. Hard landscape features such as walls, steps, paving and pathways must satisfy ergonomic demands as well as visual ones. (The design of such elements of a garden is also covered in detail in the Hunt and Whateley publication.)

The way a garden designer chooses to deal with or considers functional elements — such as pathways — provides an insight into what distinguishes conceptualist design from other forms of garden design. For example, to a conceptualist designer a path can be more than just a path.

A path can take many guises, and it can be made from one or more of a variety of both hard and soft materials. Ergonomic guidelines suggest that it should be a certain width to allow free and comfortable pedestrian flow. A path can be solely functional with form and finish determined by a need to provide the most direct and robust route between two given points. Or it can be practical and aesthetic combining function with 'pleasure' to provide an unobtrusive leisurely stroll through a picturesque landscape. Alternatively it can be straight and angular, made from identical elements, as part of a bold formal layout. The options are endless.

Idea-driven conceptualist landscape design introduces another way of considering the 'path'. The idea determines the character of the path. The idea decides what the path does, what it is made of, and what it looks like. It may even challenge ergonomic correctness. To a conceptualist designer a pathway has the potential to have poetic meaning.

For example, at Place d'Youville in Montréal, Claude Cormier considered the humble path as a means of expression, creating a patchwork of 'sidewalks' that relate to the history of the city. The choice of surface for the paths was not based on an arbitrary aesthetic decision but on what was appropriate to the type of building that they lead to: residential, cultural or institutional. Wooden decking, stone pavers, limestone slabs and poured concrete were all used for the numerous paths that veer off at different angles from the main walkway. In this conceptualist landscape the path is not just a means of access but a sentimental journey.

Place d'Youville, Montréal, 1999-2008.
Photo: Jean-François Vézina.
Designer: Claude Cormier & Associés Inc.

The Soft Landscape

The range of plants available to garden designers is extensive and limited only by climate, location and soil conditions. And even then, with some attention, an unpromising dry, shady location with poor soil in, let us say central Europe, would still support a sizeable repertoire of plants.

Faced with such choice, designers have either adopted a design aesthetic or invented one to arrive at a more limited palette. The selection of plants for a formal garden would be very different to the one required to create a naturalistic garden.

But once a choice is made, what determines the planting plan or strategy? Even with a restricted palette, decision-making can be overwhelming, especially when issues such as growth rate, plant structure, flower or foliage colour and seasonal effects are taken into account.

In my opinion the most meaningful and successful planting schemes are those dictated by a predetermined objective or idea. The seamless planting that we associate with the gardens of Wolfgang Oehme and James Van Sweden, or the well-defined blocks of single-species planting and sculpted hedges synonymous with Jacques Wirtz's organic formalism, are two worthy examples. But neither truly represents conceptualist planting design. (see Further Reading, p.102.)

Wirtz arranges and shapes plants in a contemporary interpretation of the formal garden, while the planting schemes of the Oehme and Van Sweden partnership represent a break with the past. Both are essentially 'idea' as 'style'.

In conceptualist garden design the 'idea' is unique to a given project. It is not a 'style' that can be adapted to suit other projects and the planting is guided by the same principle. The design of the planting scheme is first and foremost determined by the all-embracing idea or related ideas. Horticultural and practical necessities may modify this approach but, even so, many conceptualist garden practitioners prefer to push nature to the limits.

In 2005, artist turned garden designer, Julia Barton, was commissioned to design a 'garden installation' for a derelict county Jail, in Savannah, Georgia. The jail closed in 1979 and because of a hole in the roof weeds soon colonized the building.

Barton's idea for the garden (right) was very much based on site history. The jail's grim past and its present state of dereliction, much of it reclaimed by nature, inspired her to create a garden about confinement, redemption and freedom.

'Resurrection', Chatham County Jail, Savannah. Designer: Julia Barton

In 'Resurrection' (which also happens to the name of a variety of fern with seemingly similar powers), plants were the principal means of expression in Barton's solution to this challenging project. Using scaffolding poles and steel mesh, she created a block of eighteen 'jail cells' and in each one she planted and confined a single species of plant. These were the inmates and included 'notorious' plants such as morning glory, golden rod and ragweed.

Across from this block, on the other side of a straight pathway that ran in front of the cells, Barton created an area of 'native plants' such as mulberry and holly ferns. These were unrestrained and allowed to grow freely like the existing weeds, which had already begun the process of recovery and 'redemption'.

Conceptualist Planting

The dictionary definition of a garden states that it 'is an area of land adjoining a building usually dedicated to the growing of trees, plants and grass'.

There is a misconception that conceptual garden design has little to do with plant material and that plants when used are merely token accessories. It is certainly true that there are high-profile conceptualist landscapes without any living plants, and that many designers reject a commitment to horticulture. But to see conceptual garden and

Ranch, South of San Francisco Bay, California. Designer: Ron Lutsko.

landscape design as representing the marginalization of plants within the definition of a garden is to take a blinkered view.

In many cases the opposite has occurred with designers introducing new ways of using plants. The concept for the garden as a whole used to determine both the function and the design of the planting, giving it meaning and expression. Sometimes the planting IS the idea. It is significant that Tim Richardson includes the work of Ron Lutsko in his selection of fifty 'visionary' conceptualist designers.

Lutsko's concept is the sort which would appeal to most plant-orientated garden designers. His starting point for the solution for this rural property was not so much the site itself, but the diversity of the surrounding landscape, which included cultivated fields, meadows, rocky-outcrops and rolling hills. This natural and man-made landscape impressed Lutsko, and suggested that the design of the new garden should be about connecting with this environment; its features providing the visual ideas for the garden.

The final design is based on what can be seen from the property. Four distinct types of landscape were identified between it and the furthest hill. These were interpreted in the garden as a series of zones, the design of the one closest to the house more structured than that nearer the garden boundary. But it is the choice and style of the planting which really carries the idea.

The first zone reflects the house plan and includes a preserved rocky outcrop and a meadow carpeted with wild flowers. The second zone is a recreational lawn, its edge broken up by irregular paving stones. The third is agricultural in appearance, with regimental rows of lavender. The fourth is the garden edge and consists of native shrubs and grasses planted so as to reflect the landforms and natural vegetation of the landscape beyond.

Lutsko looked to the external landscape for his planting strategy, drawing inspiration from the variety of both natural and managed vegetation. Meadows, hedgerows and agricultural planting are either 'borrowed' or 'mimicked' as planting ideas. The regimented rows of lavender — a plant grown as both a crop and as ornamental garden shrub — provide the boldest feature of the garden.

4 THE DESIGN PROCESS

I have divided the design process into five parts, but the 'procedure' is really a chronological guideline and should not be regarded as definitive.

1. The design brief (if applicable).
2. Deciding on a strategy.
3. Gathering source material.
4. Developing the idea into a design.
5. Realizing the idea (ways of making).

The Design Brief

All garden design — with the possible exception of festival or show gardens — begins with the client brief and an objective assessment of the given site. Conceptualist garden design is no exception. But what follows is significantly different. Unlike most other design methodologies, in conceptualist design a strategy is decided upon that will lead to an idea that will determine all aspects of the design of the garden or landscape.

The brief will provide the essential parameters, the 'do's and don'ts', preferences and requirements related to the look, function and sustainability of the new garden. The importance of considering the brief fully should not be underestimated.

The brief provides direction. Let us take, for example, a hypothetical commission to transform a disused industrial wasteland into a public garden. The accompanying notes stipulate that it must be suitable for all ages, should be safe, durable and vandal-proof. The brief also informs the designer that the location of the proposed garden was once a naval shipyard. Contained in those last few words is the clue that might determine the design strategy. The design could be based on the history of the site.

Deciding on a Strategy

According to Richardson, there are a number of ways in which conceptual design 'finds physical form in landscape and garden settings', and these may be categorized broadly as 'site based, historical, visual and autobiographical'. But, while grouping potential starting points for ideas into categories is helpful in organizing a review of conceptualist design, it would be wrong to consider each as a distinct avenue of exploration.

Determining a strategy is in effect the first part of developing an idea and, in most cases with the possible exception of festival or art gardens, the answer to what direction to take will lie in the information provided by the client, by the site visit or gathered subsequently through research into either the client or the site, or both.

Information is vital, whether it be documentary, verbal or visual. Find out as much as you can by whichever method you find most appropriate. For a private garden it might necessitate asking the client biographical questions. For a commercial project, the specific nature of the business might be a place to start. For a public space, discovering more about the history of the place and its community might be useful.

To consult the 'genius of the place', or perhaps its history, is an obvious and laudable strategy for seeking a design idea, but many conceptualist garden designers regard it perfectly acceptable to import a visual idea to a given site. This does not mean that the nature of the site and the content of the brief will be ignored, only that the principal motif and source of inspiration for the garden is likely to be an external one. In the strategy for the next stage, the 'gathering' process is less direct — more lateral than logical — and rather than an isolated act, the 'gathering' might be a continuing process and part of an individual designer's personal development.

The strategy adopted may be a response to a specific challenge, but there is no reason why it should not be broader-based: a strategy that looks 'beyond the garden fence', so to speak. It must also be accepted that designers or artists might bring their own visual vocabularies or languages to the design process: for example, a love of colour, of bold shapes and forms, or new materials. Inevitably these personal preferences will inform the design strategy.

For some conceptualist designers, the importing of a personal visual repertoire is as relevant a strategy as seeking inspiration externally or from elsewhere. Some consciously seek opportunities to draw upon their own visual vocabulary and personal design ideas. For others like me, this has involved pursuing opportunities to introduce new ways of making. These strategies are less site-specific but nevertheless appropriate.

(Note that, in landscape art, 'site specific' refers to works that are intended to be unique to a particular place, and their 'meaning' is based on this relationship. My 'Two Circles in a Stone Bridge' described in the Selected Projects is one such work, p. 48-49.)

In the 'visual approach' to conceptualist design, a single or recurring motif, a pattern or just colour effects, can be the focus of a design idea. Some designers develop their own interpretations (personal), while others customize visual material from other sources (eclectic). These approaches are taken a step further when the very method of making a garden becomes the idea; usually with unorthodox and unconventional materials.

Autobiographical interpretation is a more independent approach, and is mainly associated with art-based events and installations — or one's own garden!

Below I have listed a number of avenues worth exploring when choosing a strategy. They are based on my own experience and studies of other recognized designers.

- The architecture on site or in the surrounding landscape.
- Present-day or proposed activity connected with the site or project.
- History of the site or that associated with it.
- History associated with client, biographical or other relevant details.
- Project-specific, single visual motifs associated with the project (site, client, etc).
- Import of eclectic or personal visual motifs.
- Alternative ways of making.
- Autobiographical (blank canvases).

It is worth emphasizing that these categories are used solely for convenience. They can and often do overlap.

REMEMBER: The design 'can be about anything'.

Getting Inspiration — Gathering Source Material

Inspiration may seem heaven sent, but in most cases it is the result of an exhaustive intellectual process that can be both logical and lateral. All design depends on some visual or other input to stimulate the imagination. In conceptualist design where invention is paramount, the harvesting of this 'source material' (as it is often referred to) is essential to the development of an IDEA.

The next action is to seek inspiration after establishing a strategy, that is, a chosen aspect to explore.

Seeking inspiration can be a conscious process with a methodology that involves observation and research. But it can also be subliminal and less structured. It can be 'of the moment' or an ongoing process that constantly engages the imagination. The search for an idea might also draw upon personal experiences and from already stored memories.

It should be noted that there are designers such as Ken Smith who would consider this 'gathering of source material' as irrelevant to landscape and garden design. Smith's 'inspiration' is theoretical and intellectual and more directly associated with Conceptual Art.

Site-Based (Strategy 1)

One way of searching for an idea is to adopt Alexander Pope's principle and 'consult the genius of the place', which means connecting with a site's unique spirit and ambience. Many conceptual designers claim their work is inspired primarily by what they discover on visiting the site.

The site-based approach should not be confused with a sentimental response to the locality and a desire to create a design that is in keeping with the vernacular. The aim has more to do with invention than conservation. Nor is it simply a practical response to the site's physical challenges, for example the terrain or local climate. And it is NOT just the plot of land but also its environmental and social context that is considered.

For the conceptualist garden designer, the idea for the whole garden can be inspired by what the site offers, be that man-made or natural. For some the site visit is the start of a methodical investigation; for others the process is more intuitive and less structured. In practical terms this might involve making sketches, taking photos, examining geological surveys and studying the architecture.

Present-day or Proposed Activity (Strategy 2)

A site is not always in a beautiful landscape. More often than not, the project is for a seemingly uninspiring urban setting, but if one looks hard enough, any site, anywhere, can provide the inspiration for a garden. Considering the work or business associated with the site — past, present or future — can be a fruitful starting point and a productive strategy. It is of particular relevance if the garden or landscape is intended to fulfil a specific role focused on that business or industry. It is also pertinent if the project is connected, for example, to a public service amenity such as a hospital, educational establishment or 'special need' institution.

A useful exercise is to create a picture board of all things related to the work or activity of the establishment; it might include objects, forms, shapes, images or even just colours. But when dealing with a 'business' activity of any sort, it is essential do some research, finding out verbally from the 'horse's mouth', so to speak, or from documentary evidence.

The American landscape designer Topher Delaney adopted a similar strategy when asked to design a courtyard garden for the University of San Francisco (see p. 16). She learnt that the institution played a leading role in the world of economics and trade. This prompted her to decide that it would be appropriate if this reputation informed the design idea for the courtyard. In order to give form to this notion, she needed to find the visual motifs that would best express the concept of international commerce in the context of a garden.

The visual references can be seen in the completed garden. The design of the courtyard floor centres on a large-scale version of a sinusoidal projection map of the world, created in green and blue coloured tiles, and with trade routes picked out in grey lines. Running across the whole space and seemingly under the map are the familiar black and white lines of a barcode pattern. Three-dimensional sections of the stone used for the barcode floor, become simple benches and carry inscriptions on the topic of trade, such as 'credit' and 'debit'.

The idea of 'commerce' also extends to the choice of planting. Delaney's use of fruit trees is particularly relevant as they are vital to the local agricultural economy.

Courtyard, University of San Francisco. Designer: Topher Delaney.

Historical References (Strategy 3)

As an avenue of exploration for a design idea, 'history' is as broad as it is long. It can be political, social, natural, biographical and more. It can be the recent past, or be archaeological and geological. In most cases where historical information has been used as a source of inspiration for a conceptualist garden design, it has either related to the site or the client.

Site and Social History

The location of the site can provide a rich source of material for an idea if the history of the area is explored and examined. A design developed from research into the locality's social heritage can be particularly relevant when it comes to creating a local amenity or communal space. Seeking references to the past in images and forms can bring back memories and help connect the garden with the people that will use it. It is a strategy frequently adopted by BCA Landscape of Liverpool.

Led by design partner Andy Thomson, the BCA design philosophy speaks of the importance of 'meaningful design on a local level', and many of its projects are based on local history. The company's 'gathering of information' is a planned exercise and involves speaking to locals and hearing their stories. The 'Face of Liverpool' project for a new complex in the city's former dockland drew inspiration from the lives of real people and the issues that concerned them, such as immigration.

As a result the design of this quayside garden (right) is full of historical references. Materials commonly associated with the area's industrial history, such as steel and concrete, are the preferred choice for the tall walls that define the triangular site. Angular blocks of concrete (like crane counter-weights) serve as robust seating. A large 'porthole' punched through a steel section of the wall provides a nostalgic view out to sea. The long concrete wall features a message in 'Morse Code' and is punctured by a series of conventional size glass portholes. On to these are etched portraits of the people who contributed personal stories about immigration for an accompanying booklet.

'Face of Liverpool', Docklands, Liverpool. Designer: BCA Landscape.

Client History (Strategy 4)

Biographical information offered by a client can provide a wealth of source material with which to design a domestic garden. It can also help to make sure that the design of the garden is bespoke. It may be necessary to fulfil all the practical and perhaps mundane requirements; we are all familiar with: 'low-maintenance', 'room for washing line', 'safe for kid's to play', and so on. But I suggest that it might be a more interesting garden if the traditional and conventional solutions were avoided. The row of houses may all look the same, but why should the garden? Surely it offers the opportunity for some individuality, perhaps even idiosyncrasy.

What is more the 'gathering process' can be a convivial affair; by gleaning essential and hopefully revealing information about clients over a few drinks. Biographically speaking, it can encompass their lifestyle and passions, both past and present. Historically it can be more than the story of their lives. It can be about nostalgia and memories; their yearning for the 'good old days' perhaps. Clients can provide a source of ideas that is rich in visual material. This was certainly true when I designed a garden for a family in Muswell Hill, London.

In the Biographical Odyssey (see next page), personal information offered by the client provided a wealth of source material with which to design this suburban domestic garden. The idea was to make a garden that was based on the Veale family's (although principally the husband's) life-experiences, interests and obsessions!

The gathering process, gleaning essential and hopefully revealing information, boiled down to a chat with the client over a few drinks. I learned that he once lived near the Oval Cricket ground, that he went to medical school and became a clinical psychiatrist and that he also had a thing about jungles and 'lost worlds'. Also significant was the fact that he and his wife had struggled to find a vicar prepared to 'join in Holy matrimony' a believer and an atheist (him).

Other information was of a more practical nature: A lawn for the children to play on was needed and so was a shed; the fact that 80 per cent of the existing garden space was 1.6m above ground-floor level had also to be addressed.

The next stage was to immerse myself in all matters concerning cricket, exotic places and religion. In sifting through the material I collected and my notes from the conversation with the client, I established what visual motifs could be used to determine the larger elements of the garden design and what would be best suited to the detail.

'A Biographical Odyssey' (the Veale Garden), Muswell Hill, London. Photo: Marianne Majerus. Designer: Paul Cooper. (For additional images see 'Selected Projects', pp. 64-65.)

The 'Oval' cricket pitch and the client's desire for a hidden 'lost world', a place where he could escape from the noisy urban surroundings, provided the two main landscape features in the garden and dictated the overall layout.

The 'lost world' materialized as a circular 'sunken grotto' cut into the embankment of the upper ground level next to the house, from where it is entered by a narrow passage. The feature, which included a waterfall, was constructed entirely of natural stone with small shade-tolerant plants such as ferns, squeezed into crevices. A dome-shaped iron framework supporting a vigorous climbing plant formed a canopy to provide additional shade and seclusion. The grotto was further concealed from view by the surrounding planting, which featured large-leafed, 'jungle-like' exotics, including a totally impractical gunnera — the latter on the client's insistence.

Set into the walls of the grotto were glass fronted boxes. They were intended as a witty reference to the client's medical background, and each contained a part of a sheep's skeleton; the sense of the macabre enhanced when illuminated at night. The 'lost world' experience was completed by a fog machine and a concealed sound system that emitted jungle noises.

On the garden's upper level the space was dealt with more expansively and here the cricketing theme was developed. The oval-shaped lawn dominates and serves as a play area for the children, and a customized garden shed doubles up as a cricket scoreboard. On a bench just over the lawn boundary is seated a full size, cut-out painting of a vicar sipping tea; a sight typical of many a village cricket match. The planting that surrounds the 'pitch' takes its cue from the song 'Village Green Preservation Society' by Muswell Hill old boy, and former 'Kinks' front-man, Ray Davies, and was designed to mimic the archetypal, old-fashioned English border.

Project-specific — Single Visual Motif (Strategy 5)

This approach demands a substantial amount of lateral thinking: a leap of imagination to discover a particular motif, form, shape or colour that is pertinent to a given site and design brief. It is a visual idea that belongs not just to a designer's repertoire (and recognizable as a recurring motif in their work), but one that is unique to a particular project. Claude Cormier can do this, so can 'Topotek 1'. Martha Schwartz also engages in this approach but does combine it with her own personal vocabulary.

The solutions are often witty 'one-liners' and frequently make use of a single powerful motif, sometimes repeated. The clever thing about these solutions is how surprisingly appropriate they are to the brief and the site. It is a design strategy that requires a lot of thinking 'outside the box'.

I chose this approach when commissioned to create a recreational courtyard garden in Lincoln.

The brief was to create a safe recreational environment for residents and day patients. A multi-purpose space was required that would allow for all manner of therapeutic activities. The space was a drab and uninspiring courtyard; the architecture utilitarian. Something colourful and lively was clearly needed.

My search for a recreational activity, which was both lively and 'colourful' led me to the dance; an activity enjoyed by all. It was also rich in imagery, so I soon had the visual idea that would determine every aspect of the garden: it would be based on a dance hall or ballroom.

The dancers are metal frames, shaped like figures and dressed in climbing plants: the most floriferous were confined to the billowing skirts of the 'ladies'. Follow-spot ellipses colour the dance floor — made from a rubber-based playground material — and determine the colour of the planting under the sculptures. The scene is completed with tables and chairs. (For more details see the Selected Projects, p.93.)

Imported Visual Motifs (Strategy 6)

To consult the 'genius of the place' or its history is an obvious and laudable way of gathering inspiration for a design idea, but many conceptualist garden designers regard it as perfectly acceptable to import a visual idea to a given site.

(Picture) The Hodgkinson Centre, Acute Psychiatric Unit, Lincoln County Hospital, UK. Designer: Paul Cooper.

This does not mean that the nature of the site and the content of the brief is ignored, only that the principal motif and source of inspiration for the garden is an external one. The strategy is less obvious, more lateral than logical, and rather than an isolated act the gathering of source material might be a continuing process and part of an individual designer's personal development.

Common to all aspects of the 'visual approach' to conceptualist design is the notion that a single or recurring motif, a pattern or just colour effects can be the focus of the design idea. Some designers develop their own personal vocabulary while others customize visual material from other sources. This visually-based conceptualist design can be divided broadly into two camps: 'Eclectic' (broad-based) and 'Personal' (limited but distinctive repertoire).

Eclectic

Tim Richardson regards Martha Schwartz as the designer who most represents the 'visual' approach to conceptualist garden design, particularly in her use of pattern, line and colour accompanied by the frequent use of a recurring motif. When working on a design commission, she is able to draw upon the fruits of an insatiable visual curiosity. Most significantly she looks beyond what convention would regard as appropriate for landscape design.

Martha Schwartz is certainly attracted by Pop Art, characterized by its use of brash commercial imagery and frequent repetition of a motif. Her love of contemporary culture has certainly contributed to the introduction of new and unconventional materials to the making of gardens and landscapes; the synthetic and brightly coloured, as well as the 'kitsch' are particularly favoured by Schwartz.

'POP' New Eden magazine, Issue 1 May 1999.

It is Schwartz's open-mindedness — she also maintains an admiration for the French formal garden — that makes her work so visually stimulating. The lesson to be learned is that we should all allocate time to broaden our visual vocabulary.

My own work has always been eclectic in its visual references, but I have constantly drawn upon the irreverent, disrespectful and youthful imagery of Pop Art. Its attraction to me was that it celebrated attitudes that were the antithesis of the virtues traditionally associated with garden design. Pop Art and popular culture has had a profound influence on my garden design.

Pop's interest in the mundane and commonplace, such as product packaging, confectionary, comic books and toys, influenced the choice of content for my auto-biographical 'Boys Own' garden for the Ford Motor Company (see p. 60-61), at the Chelsea Flower Show. Sweet wrappings made in ceramic littered the garden paths and a super-size paper boat and a toy footballer also featured.

I have used Pop and most recently Punk imagery to surprise, shock, and outrage, but usually within the parameters of the design brief and with the approval of the client!

Personal

Sculptors or painters may often explore a particular visual theme throughout their careers. Henry Moore, Anthony Gormley and Francis Bacon, are three British artists whose work is instantly recognizable because of this quality. Some conceptualist designers also draw inspiration from a regular source. They develop a particular interest in specific forms (animal, vegetable or mineral) and these become their signature. This is evident in the work of designers such as Vladimir Sitta in Australia and the American, Patricia Johanson.

Since 1970, all Patricia Johanson's work has been driven by a concern for environmental issues and a love of the natural world. To create her landscapes she draws regularly on a personal vocabulary of forms derived from

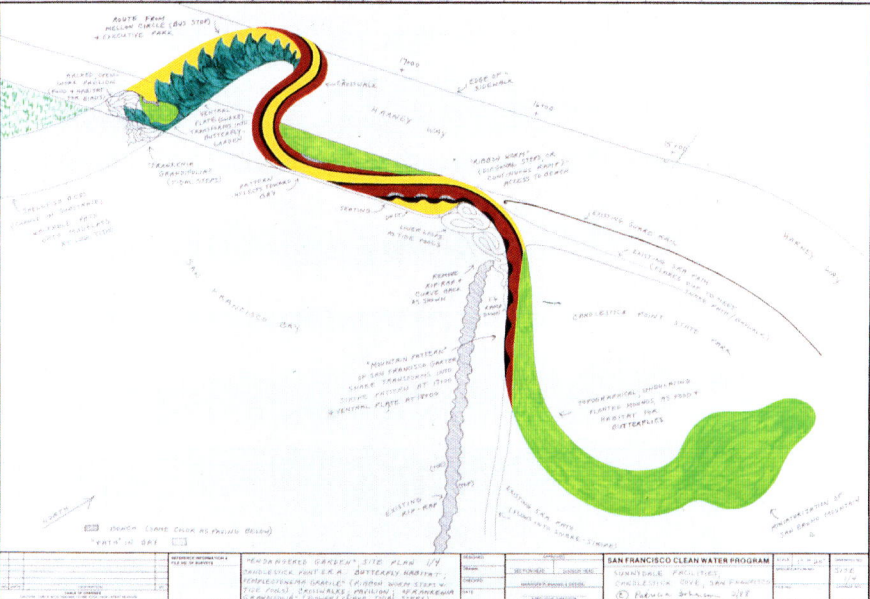

'Endangered Garden and Ribbon Worm', Candlestick Cove, San Francisco Bay. Designer: Patricia Johanson.

GETTING INSPIRATION   21

studies of plants, snakes and reptiles. But her completed commissions reveal that she also researches the history and ecology of a site.

The design brief required Johanson to improve the look of an existing sewer along the bank of Candlestick Cove in a way that would be sympathetic to the ecologically sensitive environment. Her first decision was to conceal the sewer beneath a path, in effect the path acting as a roof. For the design ideas that would subsequently determine the shape and form of this path and other landscape elements, she looked no further than the wildlife that inhabited the area.

The form of the local Garter Snake — an endangered species — is used to give shape to the walkway. The creature's head becomes an earth mound which acts as windbreak to encourage butterflies, and the snake's tail 'coils' to provide seating. Finally, at intervals along the path Johanson uses the serpentine form of ribbon worms to create a cluster of rock pools. It was a project that perfectly matched the designer's own interests.

Designers are sometimes appointed to a project because their personal 'style' is judged appropriate and applicable; some may say predictable. Others would argue that it is simply expedient. Whatever the motive the most successful solutions are those where the designer has applied his or her visual ideas within the context of the design brief.

Alternative Ways of Making (Strategy 7)

The use of contemporary materials and methods, rather than those traditionally associated with the garden, is something that I have experimented with since the nineteen-eighties. It is a recurring feature of much conceptualist design in general, and is dealt with in detail below under the heading 'Ways of Making'. But I identify it here to suggest that considering how the garden is made, and how it might 'work', can also be a legitimate and appropriate strategy in the process of establishing a design idea. In other words, the very method of construction is the idea. In practice this has manifested itself in gardens that have challenged conventional methods in favour of alternative technologies.

Autobiographical (Strategy 8)

There is another group of conceptual designers whose work is much more akin to art than garden design. The ideas that inform these gardens are an inseparable part of the designer or artist's psyche. The gardens are frequently created for festivals where the boundary between environmental art and garden design is frequently blurred.

The 'gathering process' is less tangible, the designs often based on personal experiences or on what seems to be a host of eclectic visual references; the 'Mindscapes' of the British environmental artist Tony Heywood come immediately to mind.

'The Calling', Kinsale, Ireland.
Designer: Tony Heywood.

The 'raison d'être' for the garden or landscape lies solely with the artist or designer. Not surprisingly most examples of 'conceptual gardens' by these artist-designers are to be found either at their own homes or in art exhibitions and festivals, where freedom of expression is uninhibited. However, there

'Glass Garden' (designer's own garden), Echo Park, Los Angeles. Designer: Andy Cao.

are still valuable lessons to be learned from these highly original designers. The work of the Vietnamese American Andy Cao is a case in point. His gardens demonstrate that an individual's cultural background can be a rich source of visual ideas.

His Glass Garden is unusual in that it is created almost entirely from re-cycled multi-coloured glass nuggets. The challenge facing Cao was how to design with them.

Perhaps the colour and texture of the glass jogged his memory, but Cao chose to take his inspiration from his upbringing in the agricultural region of his native Vietnam. It is his memories of this landscape that gives substance to the garden design, a series of inter-connected visual ideas superimposed upon a plan based loosely on a map of Vietnam.

To the side of the house and alongside a glass mulch path, banks of coloured glass ranging in hue from yellow to green make reference to the Vietnamese farming practice of piling up rice near the road after harvest. In the rear garden the memory of heaps of salt piled up to dry inspires the garden's most dramatic feature. Emerging from a rectangular pool is a group of conical mounds of white glass nuggets.

There are essentially two strong ideas at work in this garden. There is no doubt that the choice of material is what gives the garden its impact. It is uncertain whether Cao had originally intended to make a garden about his homeland, and that he discovered the glass as a means to achieve this end or vice versa. And even if one fails to recognize the visual references to Vietnam, the work of Andy Cao is further confirmation that the conceptualist design process can create highly original and inventive gardens.

Developing the Idea

'Design with Meaning' is the essence of conceptualist landscape and garden design. Unlike most other garden design methodologies it is not primarily a compositional exercise.

The information gathered, consciously or subliminally, visual or otherwise, will have provided the source of inspiration for an IDEA, which in turn will direct the development of the design as a whole. The idea or concept facilitates decision-making. It generates shapes, forms and structures, and chooses the colour of them. It determines how the garden is to be made and directs the planting strategy. It informs all aspects of the design process beginning in most cases at the drawing stage.

How the idea is implemented can vary from project to project, designer to designer. But it is possible to identify four principal methods:

- Working directly with the site;
- Narrative approach (the most all-embracing);
- Visual (includes emphasis on colour, new material and technologies);
- Autobiographical and art-based.

It is worth emphasizing, once again, that 'categories' are used solely for convenience. They can and often do overlap.

Working with the Site

When the idea or related ideas for a garden or landscape is based on a direct response to the characteristics of site, the process by which the idea is developed can also be direct. The working-with-the-site method tends to be intimate and respectful and is often practical rather than studio-based; which allies it closely to Land Art. Working with the site can

Sweet Farm, Eastern Townships, Québec, Canada. Designer: PLANT Architect Inc..

also mean taking an existing 'as found' landscape and making only minimal interventions. In extreme cases it is the garden-design equivalent of 'ready-made' sculpture. Many of the practitioners of this approach are environmental artists rather than garden designers. The Canadian landscape team 'Plant' is an exception.

Founding members Lisa Rapoport and Christopher Pommer believe in exploiting what they find, and are often engaged to solve problems associated with challenging sites and conditions. Their method is experiential. This is particularly true of their work at Sweet Farm (left), in the Eastern Townships of Québec, where the client's request was simply to 'help us use it more'.

After a comprehensive investigation of the site's forest landscape, Plant's solution was to make use of what was already there, including existing site debris and artefacts as well as the forest's cliffs, trees and gorges. But they would do this with minimum intervention; their aim to present it 'AS FOUND'.

First, they identified existing areas or objects of interest, adapting or adopting them accordingly. Discarded rusting mink cages became open-air rooms, and an abandoned car was retained as an art object. Elsewhere a simple projecting pier was built to extend a cliff-top path into the tree canopy, and on the forest floor a jetty was installed to render a natural pool more accessible. Finally Plant established a network of old and new pathways, most of them informal with several merely adapted deer runs, to connect all the places of interest.

This work by Plant is more strategy than design and requires the adoption of an alternative attitude to landscape design, one that is more conceptual than conceptualist. As a way of working it involves a close relationship between designers and contractors (a team effort) in all aspects of the landscape design process, one that relies on directives and on 'on-site' decision-making.

Working with the site does not have to mean abandoning the studio. Fewer hands involved — and conventional in that a design on paper is prepared — but still respecting the idea of minimum intervention, is a characteristic of the work of American landscape architect Keith Wagner.

There is an element of the 'genius of the place' in Wagner's approach to this hilltop residence (right). He chooses to use local materials and indigenous plants and, according to the designer, the response to the site is guided by the poem 'Hilltop Temple' by the Japanese poet Basho. Less obtusely, the geometry of the design reflects the footprint and axis of the house.

Hilltop Residence, Vermont, USA. Designer: Keith Wagner.

DEVELOPING THE IDEA 25

But it is Wagner's methodology that is important. The idea for the garden is based on a strategy of restraint, a sort of 'anti-design' that seeks to respect the 'as found' characteristic. Where walls are required (to establish level platforms or to provide direction), they are low and non-intrusive, and are made from local stone mimicking the vernacular fieldstone walls.

A minimal palette of moss, fern, birch, hemlock and maple provides the new vegetation. Close to the house a group of white birch trees are arranged in orderly rows, partly under-planted with expanses of fern and moss, which extend to form a buffer-zone between the house and car-parking. There are no clearly-defined borders. The rest of the planting, including maples, merges with the existing woodland.

The house is connected to the landscape by the garden's most striking feature. A reflective and luminous trough set into the ground mirrors a narrow slit window cut into the façade of the house. Obviously 'man-made' it still honours the designer's strategy of minimum intervention for maximum effect.

The Narrative Approach

A 'narrative' is probably the easiest method to digest when considering how an 'idea' might be developed and given the physical form of a garden. The narrative is rarely a story in the usual sense of the word; it does not need to be sequential with an obvious beginning or end.

The role of a narrative in the design of a garden can vary. It can be transparent, designed to be 'read' with clear visual signposts. This is often the case with 'historical' or 'biographical'-based ideas (as with 'The Veale Garden' described above under 'Seeking Inspiration'). Alternatively the meaning of the narrative can be more allusive or symbolic with the intention of engaging the client's or visitor's curiosity. In Martha Schwartz's 'Splice Garden' (right) the 'narrative' represented in the forms, colour and surfaces of the design can be interpreted as a cautionary tale on the dangers of genetic engineering.

Perhaps surprisingly, the narrative can also be used simply as a design tool, as a means of developing an idea. An awareness of the 'story' is important only to the designer, with the resulting garden to be appreciated in its own right irrespective of what it might represent. Or it can serve as both a design method and as a means of engaging the onlooker.

But in all cases the methodology is either linear or compositional. Linear is where the design is a clearly visible series of connected motifs to be 'read' almost like a conventional story. Compositional is the most common format, where the 'story' is more like a painting, with the elements that make up the garden arranged and placed according to a logic determined by the narrative.

The narrative can be a work of fiction, a biography or a history. It might make a social comment or a political point but, as with all conceptualist design, the idea expressed by the narrative dictates the design and its content, including both the hard and soft landscape.

The two contrasting projects described below illustrate just how diverse the narrative method can be, both in style and content, and in the breadth of design opportunities that it can offer.

The Splice Garden was commissioned as a contribution to an art collection by the Whitehead Institute's director David Baltimore. The work is primarily site-specific. Two factors influenced Schwartz's thought process: one was the limitation of the rooftop site; the other was the work carried out by the Institute.

The site was a 5m x 7m rooftop courtyard, surrounded by sterile high walls and overlooked by a classroom and faculty lounge with access to the space. The floor of the courtyard had a weight restriction and there was no water supply, so the use of living plants was out of the question.

Schwartz decided that since she could not use real plants her first objective was to create a sense of a planted garden by other means. She elected to use the power of suggestion: The 'plants' in the garden are all fake (made either of plastic or 'Astroturf' covered steel), and the walls of the garden are painted green.

Her second objective was to invent a narrative that would relate the 'garden' to the scientific research carried out at the Institute — notably genetic engineering.

Schwartz's narrative idea becomes a message about the dangers of tampering with nature, and the fear of creating monsters as a result of 'gene splicing', the method by which the DNA of two different entities are joined together. Finding ways of giving visual form to this cautionary tale is what drives the design of the garden.

Schwartz's solution is an essay in lateral thinking. She decided to splice together two gardens and looked to garden history for visual inspiration. A strong contrast was needed in order emphasize the 'splicing' so she chose two very different types; a French formal garden and a Japanese Zen Garden. The distinctive gardens also provided Martha Schwartz with a wide variety of forms and textures to work with.

The overall design is an uncomplicated composition. The not-quite-square space is divided diagonally into two equal parts. One side is based on the French Formal Garden, the other on the Zen Garden. A circular box 'hedge' in the French garden is truncated sharply and slightly off centre to create an imaginary pane of glass that seems to join — splice together — the two gardens.

But all is not as it should be. Elements traditionally identified with one or other of the two gardens have become mixed up.

'The Splice Garden', Whitehead Institute, Microbiology Research Center in Cambridge, Massachusetts. Designer: Martha Schwartz.

Schwartz has turned the rocks usually found in a Japanese Garden into French-style topiary spheres, and coloured the raked gravel bright grass green. In the French garden the artificial box hedges have palms and conifers 'growing' out of them. It is a garden full of irony, which can be 'read' and appreciated instantly, like a visual pun.

The Allegorical Garden (right) is further illustrated and described in 'Selected Projects' at the end of the book (pp. 56-57). Below is a stage-by-stage account of the design of the garden.

The brief presented by the clients (who had recently discovered Buddhism) was to create a garden that would engage visitors and be a talking point. The site itself was as a blank canvas: a level rectangle bounded by a rising wooded area on one side and a hedge on the other.

My strategy was to explore the client's philosophical beliefs, in particular those concerned with the origin of life on earth, and to come up with an appropriate narrative that would inform the design of the garden.

I chose to devise an 'allegory' based on the importance of water to the emergence of life and created the storyboard below:

1. The arrival of the ingredients that will form water;
2. Water is 'activated' by an external force;
3. The 'charged' water makes the 'desert' fertile;
4. Life forms develop;
5. The arrival of 'man' and the 'man-made';
6. Plant-life subjugated to the will of man.

An Allegorical Garden, Kilcot, Gloucestershire. Photo: Marianne Majerus. Designer: Paul Cooper.

The next stage was a quest for the imagery that might give visual form to each part of the narrative. The geography and culture of the Middle East, regarded by many as the kernel of civilization and the biblical 'Garden of Eden', seemed a good starting point. The search for an appropriate palette of plants was also instigated. From this point on, every aspect of the garden design, every element and every plant would be determined by the narrative idea.

The design developed as a series of events and features linked by a water course that emerge sequentially across a 'desert' of stone debris — 'a landscape devoid of life'; as a sample of my original notes suggests:

1. Fragments of stone arranged to suggest a primeval flowing (like a lava?) which mysteriously turns into water.
2. An 'oasis' / reservoir of water, circular like the earth; filled with oxygenating plants.
3. An unsophisticated device to 'activate' the water, to create ripples. Look at ancient irrigation devices? Possibly 'powered' by a natural phenomenon, such as the wind.
4. Water appears to spill out and spread / a flood plain. Area closest to 'pond' planted with moisture-dependant plants / fleshy, foliage types (hosta), gradually displaced by shrubs.
5. Regimented planting in formal beds to represent the use of plants in the service of mankind (lavender and fruits).
6. An arrangement of statuesque geometric forms: the beginning of mathematics and the emergence of a sophisticated civilization.

In this conceptualist garden, the design is the 'story' and the 'story' is the design. Yet it still functions as a garden even if one is not privy to the narrative that shaped it. The garden has all the traditional elements, a water feature, a sculpture, flowerbeds, walk-on surfaces and furniture. The visual interpretation of a 'story' is the method by which the garden is designed.

The Visual Method

This visual approach to conceptualist design usually results in a garden that has a strong and immediate visual impact, and is often characterized by the use of a clearly identifiable motif.

A common practice among designers is to create a design using an appropriate borrowed or imported visual reference. The idea can begin with just a single visual motif which is then developed into a design simply by the repetition of it within a formal framework: a tactic often used by Martha Schwartz, who also delights in discovering and employing recurring forms. Similarly shaped bagels, 'Necco' wafers and tyres ('The Citadel, Commerce, CA.) have all featured in her projects.

The process can be more complex and involve the invention of patterns, shapes or forms; or it can be simply the employment of colour.

For designers, such as Vladimir Sitta, the idea of the garden or landscape will involve bringing their own visual vocabulary or regular source of inspiration to the project.

Irrespective of whether the visual starting point is of an eclectic or personal nature, a defining feature of this approach to conceptualist design is that the designers rely heavily on their own aesthetic preferences or design philosophy. Those at 'West 8' of Rotterdam maintain that a design should stand alone with no external associations or meanings.

But whatever the 'manifesto' of the designer might be, the development of a visual idea into a coherent design for a garden or landscape will always be determined in some measure by the site — it will be 'site-specific' even if it is not site-inspired — and by the client requirements or preferences, which will either permit a personal essay — as with Johanson or Sitta — or require the application of a bespoke thought process.

As with all conceptualist design, the visual idea will have an impact on all aspects of the garden landscape, from surfaces and structures to planting. And the best way to demonstrate how a visual idea can be developed into a garden design is through examining actual projects.

Martha Schwartz is regarded as a one of the principal exponents of the visual approach to conceptualist landscape design. Her choice of visual motifs may be idiosyncratic — from bagels and gold frogs to 'Necco' wafers and Le Nôtre — but they are always pertinent to the project, as is her use of pattern, the design of which is often inspired by the site and its architecture.

Her design methodology is based on a thorough understanding of the site and the project requirements. She solves problems but the design is not a slave to the solution.

This project (right) provides an excellent insight into how Martha Schwartz develops an idea.

The site was the former location of the Uniroyal Tyre Company. When the factory was demolished it left space for a proposed mixed development of office buildings, retail mall and hotel. Significantly the developer had decided to retain the original Assyrian-temple like façade of the factory office building.

Martha Schwartz seizes on two pieces of information contained in that statement: the link with the Middle-East, and the fact that tyres were once manufactured on the site. The two 'starting points' seem literally miles apart, but Schwartz combines them to great effect.

Her overall landscape scheme is strongly suggestive of the ancient Assyrian agricultural landscapes of Mesopotamia, the remains of which reveal a ground plan based on squares. And it is this visual idea that directs how the space is organized and functions.

A powerful central plaza, around which the buildings are located, is the focus of the design idea. Schwartz's plaza takes the form of an oasis. This 'idea' determines the soft

'The Citadel', former site of Uniroyal Tyre Company, Commerce, California. Designer: Martha Schwartz.

landscaping, namely a plantation of palm trees in regimented rows. The design of the ground surface, which is a pattern of rectangular areas of grass and coloured paving, borrows again from middle-eastern influences and is used to designate pedestrian and vehicular areas.

However, Schwartz looked to a more local 'icon' when it came to detailing the landscape furniture. An oversize mock-up of a Uniroyal whitewall tyre — formed in cast concrete — is placed around the trunk of each palm tree to provide seating and protection from vehicles. The 'tyres' also replace conventional curbs as a means of directing traffic.

It is the whitewall-tyre motif coupled with the palm tree, repeated over two hundred times, that dominates the plaza and gives the former factory site an instantly recognizable, new identity.

I chose the next example, despite the fact that is neither a garden nor an outdoor space because of the processes of lateral thinking involved. It also demonstrates how a developed design philosophy can be an advantage to a conceptualist designer.

Cormier's brief was to create a winter garden within the Palais des Congrès convention centre in a section of the building that was located over a highway. The designer's response was to apply the same principle to this indoor project as he would to any external garden.

Underpinning Cormier's approach to design is a philosophy based on honesty, which includes a distrust of imitation and naturalism, and it is this that pervades his design strategy for the convention centre. The decision to reject the use of living indoor plants for the project — even though the site did not prevent them — stems from Cormier's determination to avoid artificiality.

His search for a design idea was directed by a belief that something bold and bright was required to compensate for the grey and cold of a Montreal winter. Cormier has a passion for brash synthetic colours, which he incorporates into his designs at every opportunity.

Yet, once these strategic decisions were made, how did the actual design idea evolve? Cormier looked to the city of Montreal itself for inspiration. Two very contrasting starting points define the garden. One was the city's major cosmetic industry; the other was the existing tree-lined street landscape. The strong visual impact of the final design solution is created by a fusion of both into a single motif.

Fifty-two silver maple tree trunks fixed at floor and ceiling are arranged to form an avenue. But they are not felled trees, instead each is a concrete cast of an actual tree, and each one is different. Cormier has then painted the trunks in a bright, 'cosmetic rouge pink' colour. The visual impact is immediate. It is undeniable that the sculptural design owes a debt to Pop Art — the work of Claus Oldenburg comes to mind — but this does not distract from its originality.

'Lipstick Forest', Palais des Congrès, Montréal, 1999-2002. Photo: Jean-François Vézina. Designer: Claude Cormier & Associés Inc.

DEVELOPING THE IDEA   31

A distinctive three-dimensional motif as used to great effect by Cormier is not the only type of visual idea that can be explored in the design of a garden. Light and colour, and light alone, can play a part, especially when the site in question is dark and gloomy; as was the case when I was commissioned to design a garden for clients in north London.

This 'Night Garden' garden is featured in 'Selected Projects' later in the book, but I refer to it here to demonstrate how an unusual client requirement, a less than promising site and my own interest in visual and theatrical effects led to an unconventional solution.

The clients wanted a colourful garden, but the site faced north and was full of trees – all with a preservation order – which made the garden dark and gloomy. An abundance of surface roots also restricted the planting options. In truth any new planting would struggle to become established and would have to be restricted to being ground cover tolerant of dry, shady conditions.

It was this limitation that made me consider an alternative approach to creating a colourful floral garden. I was helped by the fact that the clients, who both worked during the day, requested a garden that they could enjoy at night.

The solution was a theatrical one. In previous show gardens, I had experimented with using technology associated with the film and television industries and had discovered that back-projection screen material stood up to outdoor use. I had also investigated the use of slide-projectors. So, for this north London property I created a garden which was essentially a light show.

In the daytime the garden appears as an arrangement of twelve free-standing, white panels, all 2.4m high but varying in width from 600 to 1200mm. Constructed from back-projection cloth stretched over a timber frame, the screens play host to a shadow play on sunny days; the natural light that gets through the tree canopies created ever-changing patterns on the white fabric.

But it is at night that the idea of the garden is fully revealed. Then the dark garden is transformed into a bright and colourful one, by pictures projected on to the screens. Each image contributes to an idealistic 'virtual' garden, which the clients would love to have if only circumstances permitted. On other occasions close-up studies of flowers were projected, synchronized with single colours as part of a more abstract presentation (see illustration).

'Night Garden', North Finchley, London. Projected images: Marianne Majerus. Designer: Paul Cooper.

Autobiographical and Art-based

The type of garden referred to here is unlikely to be site-specific or be a response to a specific brief. Neither is it likely to fulfil any practical function. It is the festival garden, created as a garden for garden's sake or as art for art's sake.

These creations are distinct from the traditional show garden (most of those at the Chelsea Flower Show) which will have been funded by a sponsor, with the designer's freedom curtailed by a responsibility to the client and to a marketing message. Gardens are frequently sponsored by charities keen to increase awareness of their cause.

In all cases the designer's brief is to create a garden that will catch the eye and, most importantly, the attention of the media. Winning a medal would also be useful. To design a temporary garden with any form of brief would not be too different from creating a conventional, permanent one. Applying a conceptualist approach to the design of a show garden could of course be helpful.

Yet creating a garden with little or no parameters, save the size of the site and the budget, is a different matter. And it has to be said that the difference between what is an 'art installation', and what constitutes an 'alternative garden', is rarely clear, mainly because the way in which an idea is developed is common to both disciplines.

Within these circumstances, the decision-making is with the individual artist or creative team, and it demands a certain type of mindset. It is not something that can be easily taught. A four-year degree course in sculpture, and several years as a struggling artist provided my education. And my experience has informed some of my forays into flower shows and garden festivals. This is particularly true of 'The Greening of Industry' (Chelsea Flower Show 1992) and the later 'Heavy Metal' garden which were both re-workings of earlier sculptural projects (see 'Special Projects' below, pp. 58-59 & 84-85 respectively).

Tony Heywood's background is very different to mine: he worked as a head gardener at several private housing estates in central London before building up an impressive portfolio of 'horticultural installation art'.

None of Heywood's work is conceived in a functional way; his works exist somewhere between conceptual art and landscape design. The ideas that lead to the highly individual, colourful and bejewelled organic forms, created in a variety of unusual materials, are based on a reaction against the romantic idealistic view of nature.

He uses living organisms in his art, because it means the work will change over time and will never be resolved. He deliberately uses 'spectacular' plants because they grow like that for nature's sake and not ours. With

'The Echo', Belfast Botanic Garden, Northern Ireland. Designer: Tony Heywood.

electronic sound effects adding to the spectator's experience, Heywood describes his installations as 'mindscapes' as much as landscapes.

Ways of Making (building ideas)

These can be categorized as:

- Unconventional as opposed to the commonplace;
- Modern materials and methods;
- Theatrical and kinetic;
- Planting technologies.

I have already dealt with the direct, hands-on approach to creating a garden or landscape in the section 'Working with the Site', a method which is essentially an extension of the design process and the development of the idea.

Here I examine how conceptualist design, with it its idea-driven methodology, also determines the way a garden or landscape is made; how the idea dictates the materials and methods to be employed in the realization of a garden or landscape; and how the design of a garden can be based directly on a conceptualist strategy that seeks to employ innovative materials.

Just as clay or stone is no longer the exclusive medium for sculptors, so the conceptualist landscape designer no longer feels restricted to traditional ways of making gardens when seeking the best way to realize an idea. Technologies more commonly associated with modern architecture and interior design have been adopted by many garden designers, because of their potential to extend the creative possibilities available.

This is not to imply, however, that conceptualist design represents the wholesale rejection of traditional materials and methods in favour of new ones. On the contrary many of its practitioners use natural and man-made 'conventional' materials. Some designers are environmentally friendly and recycle waste material. What IS certain is that the IDEA will have determined what the garden is made of, and how it is constructed.

The unconventional from the commonplace — the re-working and re-assessment of traditional materials and methods

Walls are made of stone or brick, fences and trellis of timber, and the ground is covered in gravel, stone or concrete paving. These are the typical ways of dealing with familiar hard-landscape issues. Some conceptualist designers find no place for such customs in their designs. Others have re-visited materials such as wood and stone, and have discovered new ways of using them. Sometimes the material itself IS the idea, on other occasions the idea determines it.

The overall concept for West 8's design for the 'Interpolis' Garden in the centre of Tilburg (right) is based is loosely on the geological phenomenon called 'tectonic plate movement', and the large-scale materials are intended to be a foil to the garden's adjoining large office block.

One of the boldest features of the design is the treatment of the area closest to the building. Here the tectonic theme is expressed through a slate ground cover of epic proportions, so much so that the overlapping, massive fragments of slate seem to threaten the clusters of magnolias growing amongst them. Although part of an overall concept, the singular use of a material in such a striking and dramatic fashion, suggests that the very nature of the stone itself is at the heart of the idea.

On a more modest scale in every respect, the 'mixed-media' project described on page 36 is intended to demonstrate how materials and products in common use in the landscape construction industry can be re-considered in a conceptualist design context; also, to show how these conventional materials can be used to express a visual 'idea' as well as serve a practical function. (See also in 'Selected Projects', pp.52-53.)

This design for a 1930s modernist house is one of my earliest gardens. The clients did NOT want a cottage garden. They were seeking a design that reflected the style of the house, looked well from an upstairs office, and also made the garden look bigger than it actually was.

'Interpolis' Garden, Tilburg, The Netherlands. Photo: Jereon Musch. Designer: West 8 Urban Design & Landscape Architecture.

My aim was to create a design that would combine these requirements in a single, coherent whole. To devise a geometry that would echo the lines of the distinctive white house, give an illusion of depth when viewed from the ground-floor living room and be appreciated in its totality from a first floor office. There was also the client's request to consider that planting should be tidy rather than 'loose and free'.

The idea for the garden was partly inspired by a stained-glass window in the entrance hall. Although the outline of the house is predominantly rectangular, the architectural detailing used the circle as a recurring motif and this features strongly in the design of the window. Whereas the rectangle implies a state of rest, the circle suggests motion. I attempted to exploit this dichotomy in the design of the garden.

The garden also owes a debt to the work of the British artist, Ben Nicholson. His synthesis of the 'still-life' into 'constructivist' compositions based on the rectangle and the circle, encouraged me to imagine the ground plan of the garden in terms of a drawing or painting. The importance of the view from the upper-floor office window reinforced this approach.

The idea of the garden as an abstract painting required the customary patio, paths, lawn and planting to be considered in terms of line, shape, form, texture and colour. The client was keen to use tried and tested materials, so stone, concrete, brick and wood were the obvious choices for the hard-landscaping. But I was determined to employ them in a less ordinary way.

Paving to Create an Illusion

A narrow stretch of mixed hard landscaping bisects the garden to link the house with a semi-circular water feature at the end of the garden. At each end, and some distance apart, there is an area of square concrete slabs. The same type of paving is used for both, but the area near the house is covered with larger slabs than those used near the pond. When viewed from the patio doors, the perspective trick tricks the eye into believing that the paving at the rear of the garden is further away than it actually is.

Drawing with Bricks

The bricks are used as a linear device. Set in the ground and laid 'soldier' fashion, they form sections of a circumference to define a circle within a rectangular lawn. Elsewhere within the garden's geometry they are laid lengthways (stretcher fashion) and in straight lines.

Painting in Concrete and Turf

The composition is dominated by two circular areas created predominantly with grass, but with concrete incursions. One of the circular lawns is truncated by a geometric chord where the circumference cuts into the central band of paving and gravel. The remaining area of the circle is a 'cast-in-situ' slab of exposed aggregate concrete. The chord, defined as a brick line, is aligned at an angle to the adjoining section of square paving, making the circle of turf and concrete appear like a large turntable which is in the process of revolving. The chord is also angled so as to exaggerate the effects of perspective and to enhance the illusion created by the paving. A similar but larger-shaped area of concrete helps to define a circular area of lawn on the opposite side of the garden.

'Torrens' Weybridge, Surrey.
Designer: Paul Cooper.

36   THE DESIGN PROCESS

Constructivist Timbers

'Four by four' timbers are used for the construction of a three-metre high post and rail structure. The framework which is painted bright white serves two purposes. First, it extends the two-dimensional geometry of the garden into the vertical plane to connect with the architectural lines of the house. Second, it acts as decoy, the tall white framework distracting the eye from a formidable and unsightly conifer hedge on the neighbour's side of the rear boundary wall. The timber construction was not designed as a support for climbing plants; clothing it in greenery would have defeated the object.

Modern Materials and Methods

It is true to say that conceptual garden design is synonymous with the introduction of new ways of making gardens. One of the reasons why it has regularly employed new materials and methods is because the idea, rather than convention or convenience, has determined their use. Another reason is that many of the creators of these gardens have been influenced by contemporary art and other design disciplines.

Since the end of the nineteenth century, architecture has embraced all manner of innovative building techniques for functional, aesthetic and economic reasons. Steel, glass and concrete have replaced timber, stone and brick. The 'dark and satanic' has given way to the light and spatial. New construction technologies have allowed architects to design ever-more adventurous structures while at the same time enabling contractors to build them quickly.

While architects were exploiting all the exciting developments, the majority of their contemporaries in garden design and landscape architecture were busy resisting change. Modernism was adopted by a few in Europe and the USA, but in Britain it was mainly rejected. Here most customers preferred gardens that had a 'weathered and worn' look. New technology as far as the garden industry was concerned was about making concrete look like antique stone.

Only recently have attitudes changed, and the conceptualist designer's eagerness to experiment with different materials and methods, and to explore new technologies, has taken advantage of the change. In Britain the garden industry had woken up to the fact that, in order to increase market opportunities, it would have to extend its customer base and embrace contemporary lifestyles. There was a limit to the number of pieces into which the old cake could be cut.

The use of contemporary materials and methods, rather than those traditionally associated with the garden, is something that I have experimented with since the 1980s.

My 'conceptualist' gardens reveal many starting points, but fundamental to my approach is a philosophy, which when published as a manifesto in 1984, presented a challenge to the 'stick-in-the-mud' attitude to garden design that was prevalent in the UK at that time.

The manifesto was first published in *Horticulture Week*, c.1984. An edited version is reproduced here:

- Plants should not be regarded as inseparable from garden design.
- New materials and new ways of making gardens should be adopted.
- Speed is regarded as a virtue to avoid gardens becoming old before they are new. We favour youthfulness in design. Maturity and age should not be regarded as a quality.
- A garden need not be regarded as permanent. New adjectives such as instant, portable, even disposable, might be used to describe the new gardens.
- Today's gardens should be in tune with contemporary issues, style and lifestyle, and not be an attempt to recreate the past or be a sentimental, re-working of out-of-date ideas.
- Above all, today's gardens must not be without meaning. A garden should be an expression of a visual idea. So long as garden design in Britain continues to say nothing new, it will never be a voice in the dialogue of art and design.

The manifesto was the brainchild of my associate Cliff Gorman, and called for a new definition of the garden, one that reflected the spirit of the age, embraced the demands of contemporary culture and lifestyle such as social mobility, fashion and modern technology. These were issues that other design disciplines and industries had long since taken on board: exemplified by the sportswear business whose innovators gave the humble gym shoe a design makeover, and re-invented it as fashionable leisurewear, to be worn by everybody, not just athletes.

Portable and Disposable

Words such as 'instant', 'portable', 'pre-fabricated' and 'throwaway' had been attached to all manner of designed products, including buildings, since the 1950s. The manifesto suggested that it was time that this vocabulary was introduced to garden design, and that new ways of making gardens should be considered. This statement of intent concluded with a call for more 'meaningful' design, which is in effect the underlying principle of conceptualist design.

The ideas in the manifesto were translated into reality in two experimental gardens: one a show garden, the other 'made for television'. (See also in Selected Projects. pp.70-72.)

'Instant Garden', BBC Gardens by Design. Designers: Paul Cooper & Cliff Gorman.

Although the 'Instant Garden' was made for TV, its proposed purpose as a 'quick-fit' nomadic garden was not compromised in any way. The garden was a kit of easily portable, pre-fabricated parts, and included an out-of-ground planting system. It could be installed on a flat surface anywhere in an 'instant', ideal for those in temporary accommodation with only a concrete backyard for a garden.

The Instant Garden included many materials used in both the horticultural and agricultural industries. White windbreak fabric fixed to a designed-for-purpose framework replaced the usual fence, and colourful recycled rubber matting — used in pig-pens — provided a washable, hygienic floor. Synthetic fabrics developed by NASA were used to construct a high-tech greenhouse and to form 'designer' grow-bags. All the plants were sustained by a hydroponic system.

The garden was more a collection of design features than a coherent whole; it was a work in progress, a means to an end rather than an end in itself. A garden created for the Hampton Court Flower Show in the following year developed the ideas further.

The garden (right) took its name from a 1956 collage by the Pop artist Richard Hamilton: 'Just what is it that makes today's homes so different, so appealing?' Hamilton defined Pop Art as 'expendable', 'low-cost', 'mass- produced', 'youthful' and 'sexy'. In the 'Hampton Court' show garden 'flexible' and 'versatile' were added to the list of adjectives.

The easy-to-reconfigure design meant that all the elements contained within the garden could be rearranged like furnishings in an interior living space. This included the planters that could also be raised or lowered.

All the garden features were part of an integrated bolt-together, light-weight steel framework and included a high-tech summerhouse, windbreak screens and even a water garden. Water, which formed a moat around the edge of the garden, was covered with a 'walk-on' galvanized steel grill in order to maximize space.

There were references to another Pop artist in the garden. The design of a fountain was based on David Hockney's painting, 'Domestic Scene Los Angeles', which features a man taking a shower. The garden's three steel mesh palm trees were also 'borrowed' from the artist's California portfolio.

'Just what is it?' Hampton Court Flower Show. Designers: Paul Cooper & Cliff Gorman. (See also in Selected Projects', pp. 74-75.)

MODERN MATERIALS AND METHODS

'Blue Garden', Karam-West Residence, San Francisco Bay, California. Designer: Topher Delaney

A predilection for colourful synthetic products is visible in many conceptualist gardens. Plastic, 'Perspex', and recycled rubber have proved particularly popular, as have highly reflective materials such as stainless steel and glass. But it would be pointless and counter-productive to provide a 'must-have' list of materials. In conceptualist design, the choice is limitless and might just as likely include discarded items as modern building products.

Yet for some designers the choice of materials IS central to the idea. This is particularly true of the work of the American designer Topher Delaney. She is attracted by high-tech materials and the vibrant colours and interesting textures associated with them in her projects in California.

The view from this San Francisco Bay Area rooftop site (left) is dominated by the sea and the sky. It persuaded Delaney to use the colour blue as the visual idea for the garden. She uses the bold colour to unify existing elements, such as galvanized metal air vents and skylights, with newly introduced ones.

The design was dictated by the need for a lightweight solution. Delaney's answer was to furnish the garden with off-the-shelf products made from synthetic materials (such as polypropylene). These are intrinsically lighter than natural ones and most importantly are available in almost any colour. The seats are made from moulded plastic as are the free-standing planters. Both are in a matching shade of blue.

Blue neoprene rubber (used for diving suits) was cut into strips and tightly woven, to form covers that conceal the unsightly air extraction units. Artificial grass was used to transform the existing floor surface; here two shades of blue 'Astroturf' were cut into circular shapes and inlaid into a carpet of the same white material.

The advantage of many modern materials, such as plastics, is that they are intrinsically light in weight and portable, making them ideal for the challenges facing garden designers today. With ground space in cities at a premium, the roof garden has become a popular alternative, but conventional methods of garden construction are unlikely to be suitable. Furthermore, if an apartment is rented, its garden may not be required in the long term; it would be better if it were movable, and could be transferred to another home like the rest of the house furnishings when the time comes.

Theatrical and Kinetic

The use of visual references as a strategy in conceptualist garden design has already been considered. The use of vibrant colour has been identified as a visual motif in work by Delaney and Schwartz, and both these designers have benefited from adopting modern synthetic materials. Furthermore the introduction of unconventional patterns, shapes, forms and structures into the garden environment has been made possible by materials and methods not traditionally associated with the landscape industry: interior design and architecture have provided most of the techniques.

But these latter two disciplines are not the only ones that have been explored. The world of contemporary art is frequently seen to be embracing cutting-edge technology, and so are the theatre and performing arts. They have also attracted the attention of conceptualist designers, including myself, not only in the search for new ways of making gardens, but also in seeking alternative forms of expression — such as the use of sound and light — which might form the basis of a garden design idea.

That indeed was the case when I was commissioned to design a garden in a challenging space for a demanding but adventurous client in north London. (See also in Selected Projects, pp.78-79.)

'Multi-media Garden', Golders Green, London. Photo: Marianne Majerus. Designer: Paul Cooper.

The client brief

The client emphasized practicalities. Low maintenance was essential in all aspects of the garden, and should include only 'easy-to-clean' surfaces. The garden was to be considered as an extension of the interior living space, so it was important that dirt was not walked into the house; a lawn was out of the question.

In the daytime the garden would be mainly used by the children, and so a safe play area was essential, preferably with a non-abrasive surface. Only in the evening would the adults have time to appreciate the garden. It had therefore to look especially good at night. In the summer months the family would expect to dine and entertain guests outdoors. The rear of the house was totally glazed and the garden very visible so it had to look good all the time.

The site

The rear garden was not a large space. Wider than it was deep, and only the width of a modest-sized detached house, the available space was reduced further by a number of mature conifers around the perimeter of the garden. The client was eager to retain the tall trees as they provided privacy from adjoining properties.

The garden was north-facing and the height of the conifers and the three-storey property made it very gloomy. The ground level was a metre below the floor of the house; the soil was of very poor quality and contained debris from recent building work. Adding to these challenges was the fact that access was limited to a very narrow passage, no wider than a wheelbarrow.

The strategy

The idea for the garden, and the answer to the challenges presented by both the site and the client's requirements, lay in the way the garden was made. This strategy would inform all aspects of the design. I soon realized that traditional and conventional methods of construction were neither applicable nor physically possible, and that my design approach would involve seeking alternative ways to create a garden.

Finding inspiration

One starting point was my own 'Hanging Garden' from the 1991 Chelsea Flower Show (see 'Selected Projects', pp.68-69). This garden did away with ground-based landscaping in favour of construction and prefabrication to create a three-dimensional garden space. The relatively lightweight modular construction meant it was ideally suited to a site with restricted access.

It was also about making the most of limited space. The design of the garden took its cue from high-rise architecture, which suggested a vertical rather than horizontal approach. The garden took into account that, in the natural environment, plants are not confined to the ground. They can be discovered above and below us, on cliffs and in crevices.

All the plants were in pre-fabricated timber containers perched — some perilously — on a complex asymmetric timber framework, which at its highest point was two storeys high. The structure included an internal walkway as well as sitting areas.

The Chelsea garden was made of wood, but I realized that other materials would need to be introduced in the Golders Green garden in order to increase light values and to provide user-friendly surfaces. I found solutions in synthetic products, but not necessarily using them for what they were intended.

The clients' request for an open-all-hours garden suggested that lighting would have to play a large part in the design. The world of theatre and entertainment was my port of call in my search for ways of making a garden 'perform'.

The first decision was to construct the garden on stilts, to bring it up to the level of the house floor and then upwards out of the gloom to maximize both space and light. All the planting would be above ground in purpose built containers, filled with an appropriate lightweight medium and nourished by an automatic irrigation system.

The structure was designed as two storeys. The first-floor level was entered from two bridges that spanned a moat of planting. One bridge led from the kitchen-utility room to the children's play area with a ladder up to a child-size den; the other bridge spanned from the dining room to an outdoor eating area, and to the steps that led up to the 'sun terrace' on level two.

The planting was on numerous levels: below the ground floor, level with the floor, in raised planters at various heights above this, and at second-storey level. In order to increase the light value in the garden all the raised planters were clad in washable white 'Foamex' board, which also provided protection from frost.

The floor surfaces were carpeted with synthetic matting, made from recycled rubber. The material was developed for all-weather athletic tracks, but it made an ideal play surface, especially since it was available in bright colours and was washable.

The configuration and orientation of the structure, including the planting elements, was determined by the need to maximize the available natural light. Many of the aesthetic decisions regarding the garden's design were dictated by the methods and materials used, but it also borrowed from post-modern architecture, in particular the angular and asymmetric design associated with Frank O. Gehry.

A garden that would look especially good at night was an important part of the client brief, and this also influenced the shape of the structure. The white vertical surfaces of the planting units were essential to the garden's light show. Fixed at various heights and angles, the multiple surfaces were designed to 'deconstruct' large images projected on to them as part of a pre-programmed light show. Between the planters and behind the plants, back-projection screens were installed to add to the theatrical possibilities.

Pop and Op art paintings were part of a programmed sequence of images projected all over the garden's vertical surfaces. The manner of their inclusion is akin to 'sampling' in rock and pop music, in that the motif or picture is instantly recognizable, even when fragmented by the architecture of the garden. Roy Lichtenstein's comic book-inspired paintings, such as 'WHAM' were chosen because they had immediate impact, instantly changing a passive domestic space into a dynamic one.

Just as the idea of a 'performing garden' had informed the construction of the garden, so the planting was also designed with the light show in mind. Compact plants with silver or variegated leaves were the preferred choice, because they would best complement the visual effects created in the garden.

Kinetic devices and theatrical effects

These elements are not new to garden design. The sixteenth century garden at Villa d'Este, near Rome, included elaborate 'automata' — mechanical devices powered by water — such as singing birds and moving animals. But modern technology provides today's garden designers with even more scope to surprise and entertain.

A development of earlier Constructivism — the Kinetic art movement of the 1960s — saw artists exploring the sculptural potential of real, rather than implied, movement in their work. Conceptualist garden designers have also embraced this idea, turning to wind power, electronics and theatrical gadgets as an alternative to traditional garden fountains and sculptures.

At the YKK Research and Development Centre in Tokyo, Toru Mitani and colleagues used a variety of these effects.

Site/Brief

The challenge at the YKK Research and Development Centre was an elevated courtyard of some 650m^2 surrounded by a high-rise office block, an exhibition hall, café and a hotel. The landowner had requested a sculptural feature, which he wished to be visible from his company's boardroom.

Strategy

Toru Mitani rejected an approach based on traditional Japanese design with its innate symbolism in favour of a direct response to the dynamics of the site. The courtyard was windy, exposed to both the sky and the elements.

Developing the Idea

The idea for the courtyard is primarily meteorological in response to the prevailing weather conditions that affect both the building and the occupants. Mitani's bold but simple geometric design takes advantage of the fact that the garden will be seen mainly from above. The overall plan consists of a circle inscribed within a rectangle. This establishes three distinct zones, each of which contributes to the visual experience and makes direct reference to the garden's theme of being exposed to the elements.

Realization of the Idea

Mitani and Studio-on-Site combined traditional materials and modern technology to realize the idea. The circular central feature of the garden is made of slabs of black granite. The surface of this floor is kept moist and highly reflective by a watery mist sprayed by lines of sprinklers that cut across the circle. When looked down on, the dark wet granite acts as a mirror to reflect the sky and passing clouds. A delightful bonus is the mini-rainbows, which form when sunlight is refracted through the jets of mist.

The planting is also in tune with the overall concept of the garden; the circle of granite is surrounded by a grassy mound, which is topped by a ring of bamboos. These tall plants sway whenever breezes funnel through the enclosed space and give the staff in their insulated offices another indication of the weather outside.

The remaining rectangular rooftop space is paved in a pattern designed to take advantage of the multiple vantage points; what appears to be a diamond pattern from above looks like a chequerboard at eye level.

The design for the 'sculpture' encapsulates the garden. Instead of single stationary object, Mitanu has opted for a multi-element floor-based work. Forty small red mobiles are arranged in a diagonal formation. Described by the designer as 'wind fish', they 'swim' in currents of air, making visible the effects of drafts and breezes. In this way they act like weathervanes to provide the final element in the garden's up-to-the-minute guide to the local weather.

YKK Research and Development Centre, Tokyo, Japan. Designers: Toru Mitani and Studio-on-Site.

Planting Technologies

As with the adoption of new materials and methods in the construction of a garden, some conceptualist designers have explored the science and technical innovations associated with horticulture. 'Out-of-ground' growing methods offer the agricultural and food production industries the opportunity to increase yields. It also allows produce to be grown in alien environments. To a conceptualist garden designer the science of hydroponics can provide creative opportunities. One particular designer who has taken advantage of this new technology is the Frenchman Patrick Blanc.

In terms of conceptualist design most of Blanc's creations are variations on a single idea, and that is to create vertical gardens. Almost by definition 'out of ground', they are essentially living paintings.

Blanc's first public experiment with 'le mur vegetal' was at the Chaumont Garden Festival in 1992. His living wall consisted of two steeply inclined, back-to-back surfaces. These were covered with felt-like capillary matting with pockets in which a variety of plants was placed. The planting was sustained by water that constantly streamed down the face of the walls into a reservoir below. The benefits of this fusion of science, art and garden were enhanced in a later project in Paris.

The 'living wall' at the Athenaeum Hotel, London. Designer: Patrick Blanc.

At the Hotel Pershing Hall, Blanc employed a similar method to transform an ugly six-storey high wall into a garden. Here the plants were inserted into pockets within a stiff felt-like membrane just 13mm thick, and are sustained by a hydroponic system that drips nutrient-enriched water through the felt. The plants take root in the felt, strengthening the whole structure.

The Heavy Metal Garden, Taurus Crafts, Gloucestershire. Designer: Paul Cooper.

Blanc's choice of plants is based on his research into the types that grow naturally in conditions that are both shady and have poor soil. Generally he uses large foliage at the base of the vertical garden and smaller, more floriferous types towards the top, as this area gets more sun. He also uses species that require little or no soil such as epiphytes and lithophytes. But generally the planting is not unlike a conventional garden, except that the plan has to allow for the fact that the plants will turn upwards to the light as they grow. In this as in all Patrick Blanc's vertical gardens the planting composition appears random and natural-looking, which makes it look like a living version of an abstract painting.

I employed a similar hydroponic system in this garden (above) for an external wall of an art and craft gallery. The work was an essay on the conflict between nature (living plants) and the man-made environment. In this sculptural garden the vegetation is both supported and threatened by its location. (For more details, see Special Projects, pp. 84-85.)

The use of technology to support plant life in unlikely places has been pioneered not by garden designers but by scientists — Blanc is a professor of plant science — and perhaps more surprisingly by artists. And it is the latter that have contributed most to extending the horticultural boundaries of garden design. Case studies of works by these artists are unnecessary in the context of this book, but as a taster I describe a work by one of them below.

The sculptural installations that the American artist Samm Kunce devises are about the nurturing of healthy plants in the absence of natural conditions. Her 'hydroponic gardens' have supported all manner of vegetation in indoor environments totally deprived of sunlight or soil. In a work named 'Laws of Desire', Kunce persuaded grass to grow indoors on cylindrical, felt-clad clumps suspended from the ceiling of an art gallery. A visually intriguing collection of vinyl-lined reservoirs, pumps and hoses supplied water and nutrients, while halide lamps enabled photosynthesis to take place.

For further information regarding the use of living plants in contemporary art, I suggest the publication by Hatji Cantz entitled *Transplant* (edited by Barbara Nemitz); or *Living Sculpture* by Paul Cooper, published by Mitchell-Beazley, London.

5 SELECTED PROJECTS

I conclude the book with a selection of my own conceptualist garden designs. It is a body of work that spans more than 20 years, beginning in the late 1980s. It is visually very diverse — certainly eclectic — and critics might argue that it lacks a recognizable and coherent style. But this is in part due to my particular conceptualist approach to design, which is always fine-tuned to the client brief and the given site.

I rarely repeat an idea although certain aspects of my approach to garden design have become more evident as my work has developed. This is notable in my use of unconventional materials, theatrical effects and references to the world of contemporary art, where I started my career.

My philosophy is very simple. Seek to be inventive, aim to surprise and delight the client but, most importantly, make gardens that have meaning.

I have grouped the projects by category:

1 Site Specific

Two Circles in a Stone Bridge
Grizedale Forest proposal
Roof Garden
Garden at Torrens
A Garden Room

2 Narrative based:

An Allegorical Garden
The Greening of Industry
A Boy's Own Garden
A Football Fantasy
A Biographical Odyssey
Ocean to a Garden

3 New ways of making:

The Hanging Garden of Chelsea
The Instant Garden
The Floating Garden
Just What is It?
The Cool and Sexy Garden
The Multi-Media Garden
The Night Garden

4 The Garden as Art:

The Ford 'Carden'
The Heavy Metal Garden
The Rothko Garden
The Prism Garden
The Climate Cases
The Eden Laboratory

5 Specialist:

The Square Dance Garden
The Sensory Garden

Two Circles in a Stone Bridge

1983

A site-specific work created in the disused Tout Quarry at Portland Bill. The location was a gully that ran east to west, from the quarry to a view over Chesil Beach and the sea beyond. The architectural sculpture was built entirely in dry stone using debris from the quarry workings.

The view seaward through the circular aperture captured the sun setting around the time of the vernal equinox. Set into the top of the wall, the upper circle of stone was designed to echo the sun dipping below the distant horizon.

Portland Cliff-top Sculpture Park, Dorset
Now Destroyed

The proposal won a bursary from the 'Portland Cliff-Top Sculpture Trust' and was constructed by myself and students of the University of Lancaster. Above right: A flight of dry-stone steps was constructed to allow easy access from the quarry floor to the site.

Grizedale Forest Sculpture Trail: Proposal (not completed) 1984

This site-specific work was also to have been constructed using the dry-stone technique. Intended to suggest a fossilized industrial working, it was abandoned because of illness. The sculptural motif was to reappear several years later in a different guise in a Chelsea Flower Show Garden.

Roof Garden   A Chelsea Mews Property, London   2001

Photos: Marianne Majerus.

Measuring 2 x 4 m this very small roof garden had to be a continuation of the adjacent living space. The design also had to avoid encroaching on the limited space. Putting the traditional content of a garden — plants and fountains — and new features such as sound systems in a vertical feature was central to the idea. In order to leave as much of the floor space free of clutter, it seemed sensible to make use of the neighbouring wall. A false façade was built on to it to accommodate planting, seating and a sound system. It even included a waterfall which descended down three panels of textured glass set into the fake wall. The recesses mirrored similar features in the opposite internal wall, thereby linking the outside with the inside.

Garden at 'Torrens' — 1990

This 1930s-style property demanded a garden to match. The result was an essay in modernism inspired by the vernacular white walls and geometric architectural language of the house. The predominant use of the circle in the garden echoes its use as a recurring motif in the design of a number of the building's features. The most pressing objective was to make the relatively small garden look bigger. It was originally large but had been reduced in depth when a section was sold as a building plot. The very tall conifer hedge in the neighbouring garden remains a legacy of the sale.

1930s-Style Property   Weybridge, Surrey

The view from the living room (left) reveals the optical illusion that has succeeded in making the garden appear longer — different size paving slabs were used to exaggerate the convergence of the perspective to give a false sense of distance. I was unable to mask the ugly conifers, so a tall white framework was introduced in front of them. The white structure was designed to distract the eye rather than conceal. The view from upstairs windows was regarded as important and the treatment of the 'floor-scape' reveals the influence of paintings by Ben Nicholson; except that here deliberate misalignments in the circular pattern are intended to suggest a sense of movement, and the lawn and planting are an integral part of the composition.

A Garden Room

2001

In order to provide an additional communal area for guests, the proprietor of the hotel decided to include a roof garden as part of renovation works. The client had decided that the easiest way to accommodate such a garden would be to allocate one of the new top floor rooms and simply leave the roof off. Was it a room or a roof garden? This ambiguity and uncertainty, reinforced by a sash window in the wall overlooking the street, was something worth exploiting, and became the focus of the design. To develop the idea of ambiguity and to add to the confusion between inside and outside, I decided to include features that one would normally associate with the interior of a hotel; except that in the garden the fittings and furnishings would have to withstand the elements. It was important that the design of the 'garden room' should remain in keeping with the style and look of the hotel's Edwardian interior.

The Leonard Hotel

Mayfair, London

Photos: Marianne Majerus.

Polished limestone was used for the floor and for the fitted seating. Fragrant lavender was planted in concealed containers behind the glass back rests. Vertical surfaces were finished in brushed stainless steel. Five stainless steel column-like structures were placed symmetrically around the room on top of the plant containers to serve as supports for scented climbing plants. Works of art featured in most of the guest rooms, so weatherproof paintings were hung from the garden walls to add to the visual deception. The remaining wall surface was clad with steel mesh to encourage evergreen climbing plants to form a 'living-wallpaper' that would complete the transformation of the small space into a truly 'green' room.

An Allegorical Garden   1989

The design of this garden was determined by a narrative; a mythological and pseudo-scientific story that reveals how water became the essential catalyst in the emergence of life. A meandering 'path' of slate fragments set on edge, begins at the foot of a sculpture of Aquarius, the water bearer. Gradually and mysteriously it transforms into a shallow stream as it nears a circular pond where two stones are suspended just above the surface of the pool by a pair of carefully balanced steel arms.

Kilcot, Gloucestershire

Photos: Marianne Majerus.

The slightest breeze makes the stones raise up and down, kissing the water surface to create rings of radiating waves. As the waves strike the far side of the pool they appear to overflow. Here the spillage has seemingly created an area of lush foliage plants, which spread out from the pond to colonize a lifeless area of gravel. Further from the water source the planting becomes more structural and managed as sculptural geometric forms suggest the arrival of a human presence.

The Greening of Industry 1992

This garden won a gold medal and the prestigious sword of honour for best garden at the RHS Chelsea Flower Show. It was inspired by two places I had visited in Wales. One was an old slate quarry in North Wales, the other a waterfall called 'Water Breaks its Neck' near my home. But the garden also drew upon earlier sculptural ideas. The central feature was similar to an uncompleted proposal for the Grizedale Sculpture Trail and to a free-standing work called 'Pithead' (model shown far right), also not realized.

RHS Chelsea Flower Show

Pan Britannica Industries

The garden was an unsentimental comment on the way nature is able to reclaim the remains of our industrial heritage. Although many visitors mistook it for a real relic, the structure was not an imitation. Neither was it a miniaturisation. Instead it was a synthesis of the elements associated with the mining industry and featured reclaimed materials including rusting ironwork, chains and pulleys. Indigenous plants have taken hold and a waterfall, which appears to have cut into the structure, continues the process of demolition.

GREENING OF INDUSTRY

A Boy's Own Garden

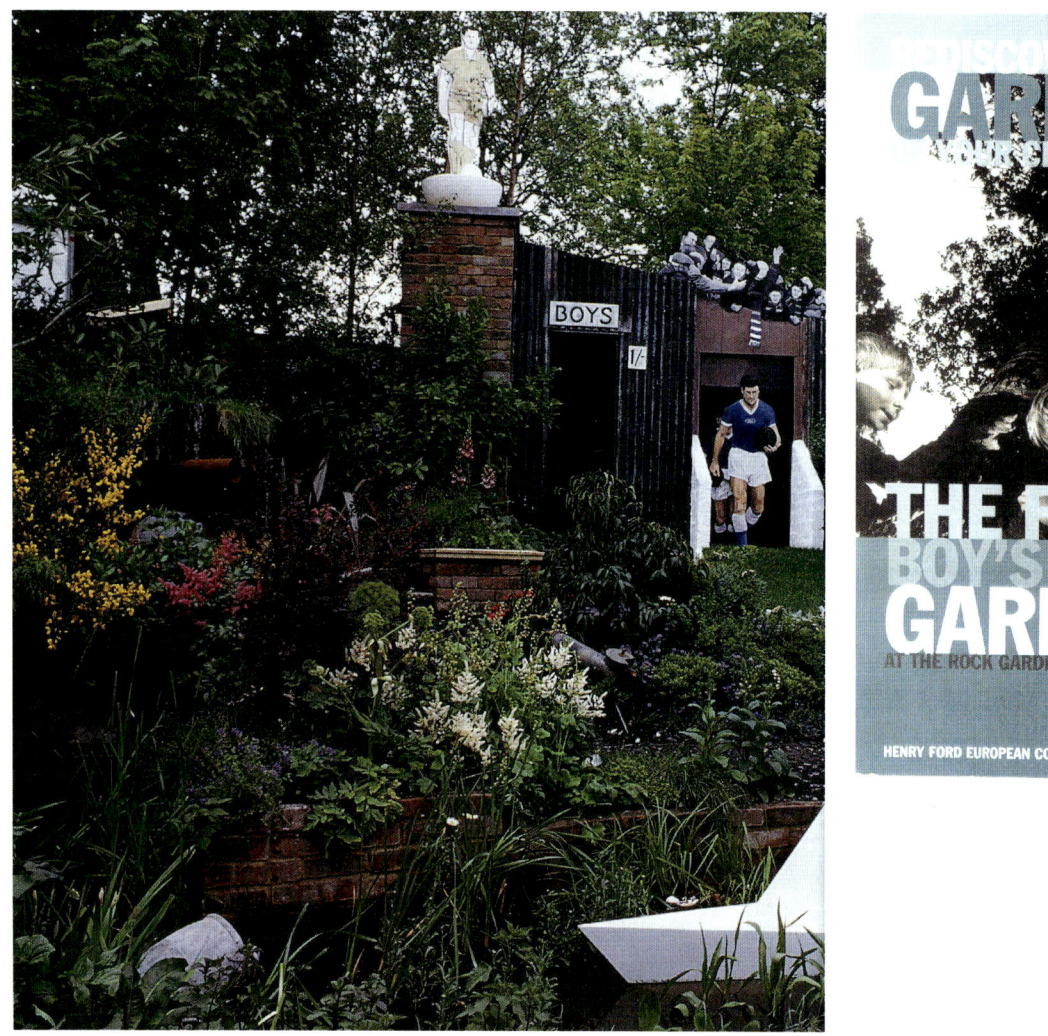

1998

Students from Central St.Martin's College in London contributed to this autobiographical garden about my childhood. With stinging nettles and other weeds, a beck full of discarded hardware and a corrugated iron den, it might be best described as a 'Grunge' garden, inspired by artists such as George Fullard and Peter Blake. It was an essay in nostalgia with memories exaggerated and frozen in time. There was an oversize paper boat and a 'Subbuteo' football player. There were discarded sweet wrappers (made in ceramic) littering the pathways and a sculpture of my first girlfriend; all set against an inside-outside football scene.

The RHS Chelsea Flower Show   The Ford Motor Company

A BOY'S OWN GARDEN

A Football Fantasy

1999

The client who commissioned this garden had seen 'The Boy's Own Garden' at the Chelsea Flower Show the previous year. His brief was to enliven a challenging urban garden space bordered on two sides by a builder's yard and a school. Most importantly he wanted a garden that was a place for him and his son to play football. A conventional garden with flowerbeds was not an option, but he did need a large shed as an extra utility room. I realized that football imagery would provide the main source of visual reference for this garden, but incorporating a shed was a challenge. Surprisingly, inspiration came from the Italian Renaissance garden, and the architectural features such as the nymphaeum at the Villa Aldobrandini. It suggested that the utility room could be concealed behind a folly-like football façade. It would also leave plenty of room for the pitch!

Battersea, London

Private Residence

In the design, the shed became the focus of attention; dressed up as a football ground, complete with turnstile, player's tunnel and crowd. It was made deliberately tall to provide privacy from the adjoining school and included a large screen on to which live TV coverage of matches could be projected. A 'dug-out' made of Perspex and pitch-side advertisement hoardings completed the scene.

A Biographical Odyssey

1997

The design of this north London garden was driven by past and present autobiographical details supplied by the client. The oval lawn, on the garden's upper level, complete with a life-size cut-out of a spectator and a shed customized with a scoreboard, is a reference to where the client lived as a child, which was close to the Oval cricket ground. The spectator, just visible in the top right corner of the image to the left, wears the recognizable attire of a member of the cloth.

Muswell Hill, London

Private Residence

Photos: Marianne Majerus.

The client, a convinced atheist, had a particular and personal reason for honouring a vicar. The client's love of the mysterious and the bizarre was catered for by a sunken grotto. Complete with a sound system to play jungle sound-effects, coloured lighting and a smoke machine, it represented the ultimate in escapism. Boxes in the stone retaining-walls of the grotto contained bones — he was a doctor by profession! A waterfall and exotic plants completed the experience.

Ocean to a Garden

2008

This garden from a more recent Chelsea Flower Show exhibit also has design based on a narrative: one closely linked to the origin of the limestone provided by the garden's sponsor 'Testi Fratelli', a company renowned for supplying high-quality stone. The history of the landscape of northern Italy began under the ocean, and the idea of the garden was to tell that story.

The history of the landscape of northern Italy began under the ocean. Over the centuries geological activity forced the sedimentary rock upwards to form mountains, which in turn have provided a vital supply of building materials. Elsewhere they have created the rich soils now colonized by vegetation.

66 NARRATIVE BASED PROJECTS

RHS Chelsea Flower Show

Simply Italian and Testi Fratelli

The stone was used to create great architecture and gardens; the architectural style of the garden refers to the sixteenth century 'Veneto Villas' designed by Palladio. The lines of saturated timbers emerging from the garden's flooded floor also made reference to nearby Venice and the efforts to create a city in the sea.

It was a garden of two levels: a lower zone given over to water, and an upper zone dominated by planting. The water columns and wave-like motif on the vertical surfaces connected the two environments. The flight of steps that lead up from the water was intended to symbolize the geological journey of the stone.

The Hanging Garden of Chelsea   1991

My first Chelsea Flower Show garden was designed to challenge the conventional way of building a garden. The show lasts less than a week, so it seemed appropriate to create a garden that was reusable. A semi- prefabricated, modular structure that could be bolted together was the answer. All the planting was confined to containers perched (some perilously) on a timber framework.

RHS Chelsea Flower Show

Pan Britannica Industries

The other aim of the garden was to present planting in a more dynamic manner than is usual. In nature, plants grow in a landscape that is far from two-dimensional, on rocky escarpments, cliff-tops and in deep crevices. Here the planting was presented not only at your feet, but above you, beside you and below you. The design also suggested a solution for gardens where space is limited. Why not think vertical and build upwards?

The Instant Garden

1989

This garden, produced for the BBC series 'Gardens by Design', was the culmination of years of research by my associate Cliff Gorman who believed that there must be other ways of making gardens. He had discovered that there were many new materials available that could be used and which could alter both the appearance and use of gardens. Above are a collage and a model dating from 1984, which attempted to give a visual impression of how the new modern garden might look and included the use of synthetic flooring, out-of-ground growing systems and windbreak fabrics to replace old style fencing.

'Gardens by Design'   BBC television production

Above left is the original model for the 'Instant Garden', which was created in a car park under the watchful eyes of the TV cameras. It was intended as a garden that could be installed anywhere, in a concrete backyard or on a roof; ideal for rented accommodation, as it was designed to be portable. Features included recycled plastic matting as a floor surface, which was non-abrasive and available in bright colours, hydroponically maintained planting and weather-resistant, fabric planters. The garden was 'wrapped' in a semi-opaque windbreak.

The Instant Garden   continued

The garden in the process of being filmed. Cliff Gorman, who originated the concept of this radical new way of making gardens, is seated on the left.

The recycled plastic floor covering is more user-friendly than old fashioned stone or concrete slabs. It is less arduous to put down, easy to enlarge, safe for children to play on and great for simply relaxing.

72   NEW WAYS OF MAKING

The Floating Garden   The RHS Chelsea Flower Show   1999

The 'Floating Garden' concept was first developed as a winter garden for a palace in Dubai. The project was cancelled, but the idea was resurrected at a Chelsea Flower Show. With the intended location for the garden being the Middle East, its original design had taken as its inspiration the biblical story of Moses floating in basket of reeds. Subsequently the design became more 'high-tech' with floating planters, powered by wind and water currents, providing a kinetic alternative to the traditional English garden of borders and beds; the relationship between one group of plants and another in constant flux. Furthermore by adjusting the depth to which the floating islands sat in the water, they could be adapted to accommodate both wet and dry-loving plants. Plants needing a specific soil pH could also be catered for when isolated in containers.

Just what is it? 1989

This garden was made in the same year as the 'Instant Garden', and was created for the inaugural Hampton Court Flower Show. The title is an abridged version of that for the Pop Art collage by the artist Richard Hamilton called 'Just what is it that makes today's homes so different, so appealing?' It seemed appropriate for a design that set out to challenge the definition of a garden. The idea was to take words such as 'instant', 'prefabricated', 'flexible' and 'portable', common to other design disciplines, and apply them to the garden.

Hampton Court Flower Show   Jardinerie Garden Centres

There were other Pop Art references in this 'pop-up' garden. The cut-out of a man taking a shower was a copy of a David Hockney painting, except that the shower fixture was real. It was the garden's water feature. The steel palm trees were also based on work by Hockney. The garden was modular with interchangeable deck sections and planting units. Metal grids (see right) covered a continuous trough of water that acted like a moat around the garden to accommodate aquatic plants and fish.

Cool and Sexy Garden   1994

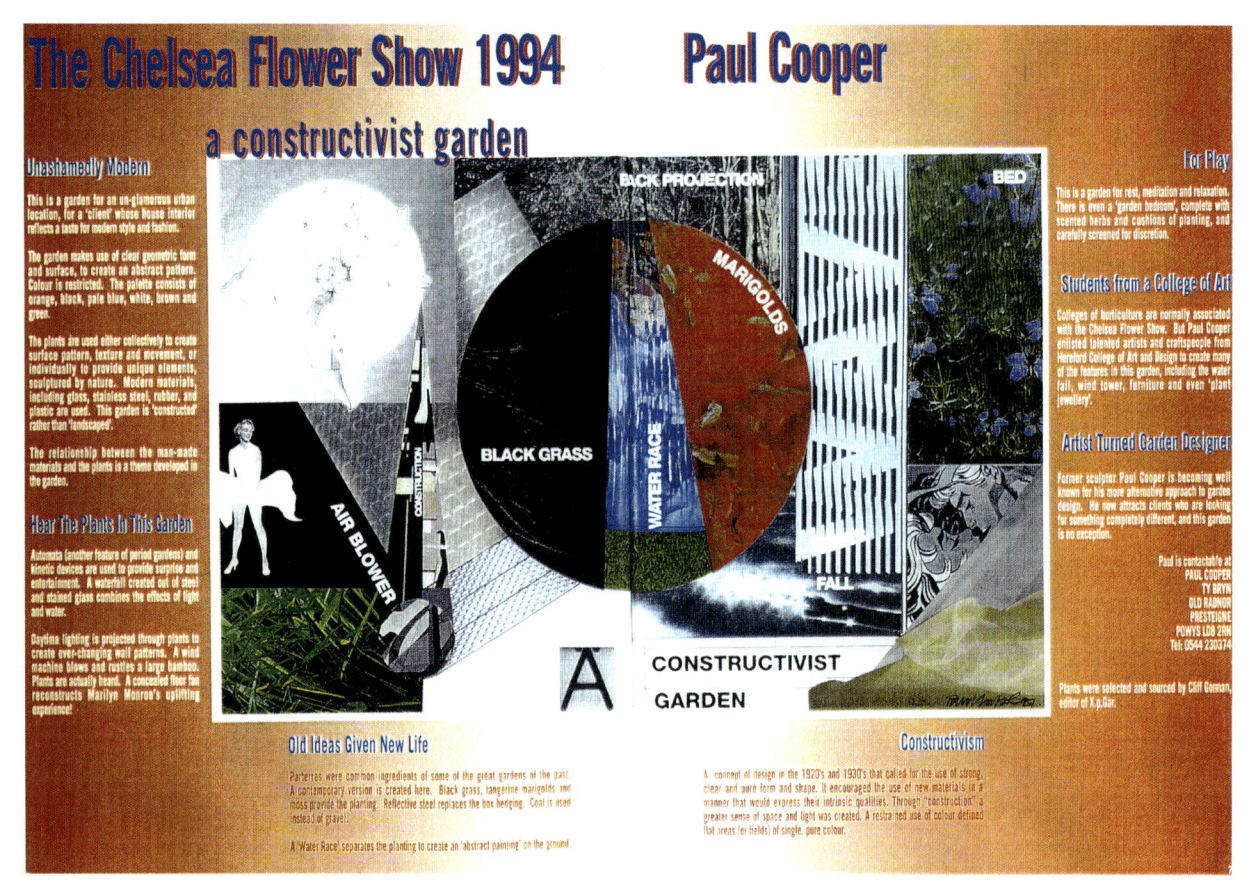

The collage above reveals that the final title for this Chelsea Flower Show garden was different to that which was originally proposed. This is one of several reasons why this garden was controversial, and why no medal was awarded. Such was the alleged shocking content of the garden that it twice made the front page of *The Times* newspaper. The design took the idea of the earlier 'Just what is it?' garden a step further. The design was over-loaded with visual ideas and effects, but the overriding idea and intent was to shock. The notoriously conservative Chelsea Flower Show was the perfect place to achieve that effect. As the author, John Le Carré once said, 'the cat sat on the mat is a statement, the cat sat on the dog's mat is a story!'

The RHS Chelsea Flower Show   Supported by X P Gar magazine

This time the garden was given sex appeal! It featured an outdoor bed, a concealed wind machine to re-create the famous Marylyn Munro air vent scene, and tree decorations that displayed erotic images. In the centre of the garden was a modern day 'parterre', which was given the punk treatment with black grass, coal, moss and marigolds. 'Shadow show' screens completed the 'X-rated' entertainment.

COOL AND SEXY GARDEN   77

Multi-Media Garden

1994

A garden designed to be enjoyed at night as much as day; this multi-level design also made the most of a problematic small and gloomy north-facing plot. The space was surrounded by tall conifers, essential for privacy but not good for other vegetation. The idea for the design was forged by the realization that the garden would have to be made in a manner that was different to traditional methods. It would have to be constructed rather than landscaped, but the design allowed for theatrical effects including projected images which at night would 'de-construct' the architecture of the garden. The garden was built on stilts to elevate the decking to ground-floor level, and to lift the planting towards the light. The planting is in raised containers set at a number of different levels, and there is also an upper sitting area. A children's playhouse is accessed by a child-only ladder. The client's main objective was to have a garden that looked good at night; he worked long hours.

Golders Green, North London

Private Residence

Photos: Marianne Majerus.

The architectural forms of the garden were clad in a white insulation board and back-projection screens filled voids. At night the garden was visually deconstructed and transformed by projected images (above: A Roy Lichtenstein Pop Art painting works particularly well). Even the planting was chosen with these effects in mind. Those with variegated leaves or silver foliage were the obvious choice.

The Night Garden

1996

This north London garden was gloomy even in summer because of the overhanging trees, which could not be removed because of a preservation order. Also, the clients both worked, so a garden that looked good at night was a priority. In both circumstances 'darkness' was the issue, and it was this that made me consider an alternative approach to creating a garden. My idea was simply to add light to improve the garden by day and, most importantly to provide a visual experience at night. The solution was theatrical.

North London — Private Residence

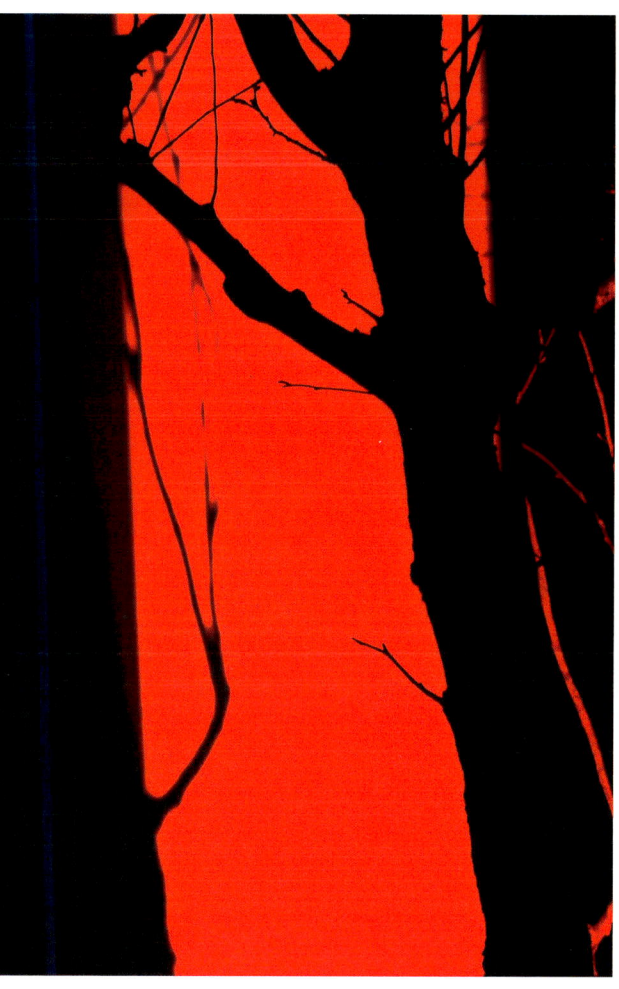

Projected images: Marianne Majerus.

The design of the garden was a simple composition consisting of two square areas of grass separated by a rectangular pool of water that divided the plot in two. A low wall was introduced along the length of the garden, close to the south-facing boundary, to create a raised bed (the only area not heavily shaded). A water feature was built into the wall where it backed on to the pool. But the main feature of the garden was the free-standing projection screens. In the daytime the white obelisks served to lighten and define the space. At night they were part of a light show. Computer-programmed projectors illuminated them in an ever-changing display, which included combining floral images to create a garden within a garden.

The FORD 'Carden' 1995

This garden was commissioned by the Ford Motor Company for The BBC Gardener's World Live event at the NEC Birmingham, as part of the launch of a new people carrier. During a visit to the Ford plant at Dagenham, I discovered that the company had to scrap piles of brand new car parts, including metal panels and welded frames during the research and development stage of a new vehicle. In the scrap-yards, the huge stacks of these odd shapes were reminiscent of the surrealistic painter Max Ernst's work, and led to the idea of creating a garden landscape, a sort of futuristic rockery. The result was nicknamed a 'carden' and was made entirely of car parts welded together into a three-dimensional walk-through sculpture.

BBC Gardener's World Live, NEC, Birmingham   Ford Motor Company

The metal forms were coated with a resin-based, high-build, textured paint and, once planted, the whole structure took on the appearance of a rock garden, complete with grottoes and customary waterfall. To exploit the 'pun' in the garden's title further, the area around the water fall was filled with 'car'-nivorous plants.

The Heavy Metal Garden

2003

Visual similarities suggest this vertical wall garden was a re-working of an earlier sculpture but the message it conveyed was very different. This work was about the strained relationship between plants and the man-made environment. In this sculpture the vegetation is both supported and threatened by its location.

Living Art Project   'Taurus', Gloucestershire

The plants, in soft containers (watered and fed automatically) were supported on the wall by pressure. They owed their existence, high off the ground, to the steel clamps that held and squeezed them. Some of the plants were forced to grow upside down! Without the steel bars and bolts, the plants would have tumbled to the ground. Unable to take root on the concrete floor below they would have perished. The steel that threatened them also sustained them. The lavender in the central square was chosen because of its sentimental and chocolate-boxy associations; the cornus because of its winter, 'blood red' stems. Taking a cue from the manner by which ancient Egyptian artists represented reality the cornus were seen in profile (some upside down) while the lavender (in the centre) was presented as if viewed from above.

The Rothko Garden   Camden, north London   Private residence   2003

Photos: Marianne Majerus.

This was really two gardens in one. The walls and paving were part of an earlier design and build which was terminated when the clients parted company acrimoniously. The Rothko 'installation' was initially created for a party organized by the wife as a way of celebration. She was a fan of the American artist and hanging this homage to him on the bare brick walls seemed an ideal solution. The planting, by designer Bonita Bulaitis, was chosen to complement the colour theme. The idea demonstrates how the introduction of an unlikely but nevertheless relevant visual motif in the form of weatherproofed paintings can provide an instant effect.

The Prism Garden   Installation   Retail Outlet, Chelsea, London   2004

Commissioned by a garden and accessory shop in Chelsea, the temporary garden was to occupy a very small central space in an exterior retail area to the rear of the building. It was obvious that something bold was needed to compete with the cluttered environment, and that height would be an advantage. The products on display were very traditional and monochromatic, mainly terracotta or wooden. To be eye-catching the installation needed to be colourful, and the idea developed from this starting-point. The temporary garden installation featured lamium, silver birch trees and ferns (planting design by Bonita Bulaitis) set within a zig-zag arrangement of vertical 'Perspex' screens each representing one of the colours of the rainbow.

The Climate Cases   2003

Photo: Marianne Majerus.

The design strategy for this installation for a bespoke conservatory company at The Chelsea Flower Show was an obvious one: glass would be an important element. The link between the glass and the garden is usually the greenhouse, but I decided to investigate this association further. The idea was inspired by the 'Wardian Case', named after Nathaniel Bagshaw Ward who discovered the principle that a sealed glass case could form a self-sustaining environment for the transport of plants, since the water transpired by the plants condensed inside the case and was re-used.

The RHS Chelsea Flower Show   Conservatory manufacturer's garden

The installation consisted of four, 1800mm high x 600mm glass cases positioned in two identical pools. The open end of each case was submerged in the water. Within each sealed 'greenhouse' was placed a papyrus, a tropical marshland plant. Concealed water pumps sprayed a fine mist into the cases. Inside each case the water condensed as it made contact with the glass, dribbling down the panes like rainwater and partially obscuring the plants. On sunny days the fine spray of water formed rainbows. The plants in the glass case only received air via the circulating water.

The Eden Laboratory (an experimental garden)   2002

Photo: Jean-Claude Hurni.

The idea was inspired by drawings in a very old biology textbook. The book illustrated various experiments involving plant behaviour and growth. Gardeners and agriculturalists alike have long been interested in influencing the way a plant grows. This garden was devoted to experiment and the science of plants rather than the art of the garden. The design of the garden was intended to mimic a research establishment, complete with security fencing, and aimed to serve as a satirical reminder of our obsession with a desire to control and harness nature for our own gain.

Métis International Garden Festival   Grand-Métis, Québec

Photos: Jean-Claude Hurni.

A

B

For example, it is often considered necessary to make a plant flower early for show purposes or to make it more productive as a food source. The RHS Gardens at Wisley have trial beds to compare the merits of various garden plants. Research establishments go one step further. Agricultural scientists experiment with genetic engineering to modify disease resistance and yields.

All the plants used could be classed as productive and all except the willow are grown as a food source.
The experiments included an attempt to see if phototropism (the effect of light) could overcome the effect of geo-tropism (gravity). A hazel was planted upside down facing a mirror (A). The answer was NO.

Another experiment was a re-assessment of an actual Victorian idea, which involved an attempt to persuade plants to grow faster by using a mechanism that would pull the growing tip upwards (B).

THE EDEN LABORATORY

The Eden Laboratory   continued

C

Photos: Jean-Claude Hurni.

D

Experiment C involved the planting of wheat seed in nine cloches. In all except one, coloured filters were attached to restrict the light available to the plants. The strongest growth was found in those predominantly exposed to red light.
Experiment D had willows planted in perforated pots above water reservoirs to see if root growth could be encouraged.

The Square Dance Garden
Lincoln County Hospital
Hodgkinson Psychiatric Unit   1994

The brief was to create a safe recreational environment for the residents. The multi-purpose space allowed for all manner of therapeutic activities but was designed around the idea of a dance hall; dancing being something that can be enjoyed by all. The metal frames, shaped like figures are dressed in climbing plants. The most colourful and floriferous confined to the billowing skirts of the ladies. The dance floor was made of a synthetic play surface, and under-planted the sculptures, and was enlivened by follow-spot ellipses.

Sensory Garden

2004

This garden was created for a home that catered for the care of adults with autism. It was important that the garden could engage the residents, so interactive features were the agreed solution. It was to become one of my most challenging and elaborate gardens. The idea for the garden came about by accident. I had noticed the way a group of autistic teenagers had reacted enthusiastically to an exhibition of avant-garde art which I was also visiting, and so decided to create a similar experience in the garden at Newbus Grange.

Sensory Garden

Newbus Grange, Darlington

In the 'Listening Gallery' the percussion sculptures, with their tubular bell skirts and colourful, maracas-like necklaces were intended to be played, as were the rows of bicycle horns or hooters (see opposite) fixed to the screens. Even the plants, notably the quaking grass (*Briza*), made a noise.

Sensory Garden — continued

Light and colour seeing gallery

Texture and touchy gallery

Sound play and listen gallery

The garden was designed like an Art museum with four 'galleries', each dedicated to one of the senses. In a fifth gallery in the centre of the garden was a simple maze of tall, coloured-Perspex screens. Each gallery featured three identical sculptures and four picture frames containing an interactive sensory feature. The sculptures shared a similar figure-like design; they were inspired by costumes created by the Bauhaus artist Oskar Schlemmer for his 'Triadic Ballet'. Each consisted of three conical forms, representing the legs, torso and head respectively. In the 'Seeing Gallery' (left), they are mirrored to take on the guise of the onlooker.

Sensory Garden   continued

Hooters in the listening gallery

Touch & feel screens are complemented by plants that encourage touch

In the 'Smelling Gallery' the emphasis was on scent. Here the sculptures were supports for fragrant climbing plants and the gallery's long border featured scented roses in a bed of lavenders. The picture frames resembled a cosmetic display with simulated perfume bottles; designed to stimulate memories of similar sensory experiences. The three sculptures in the 'Touchy-Feely' gallery, although identical in form and shape, were very different to the touch. One was covered with artificial grass whilst another was shiny and metallic.

Sensory Garden   continued

The frames in the 'Touch-Feely' gallery consisted of many colourful electric cable ties attached to panels of painted expanded steel mesh. They were designed to encourage and withstand more robust interaction than the other features did. They sat alongside a border of plants chosen for their textural properties, from leathery or fleshy leaves to brittle flower heads — a part of the garden which would also look good in winter.

Sensory Garden continued

The 'Seeing Gallery' made much use of mirrors. The picture frames, as well as the sculptures, also explored the possibilities of reflected images. In the frames (above) each mirror could be rotated 360 degrees allowing participants to engage with the feature to create 'pictures' from multiple images of the surroundings and themselves.

Sensory Garden   continued

The 'Rainbow Maze' was the fifth and final gallery. People suffering with autism require clear and unambiguous direction, so the route through the labyrinth was straight forward. What was less predictable was the visual experience when visitors saw the world about them through coloured filters, sometimes singularly but more often collectively, as the primary colours of the tall screens mixed optically to create all the colours of the rainbow.

Sensory Garden   continued

A view from within the 'Rainbow Maze' towards the care home. The colours red, orange, yellow, green, blue, indigo and violet are clearly visible.

Further Reading

Abrioux, Y. (1994) *Ian Hamilton Finlay – A Visual Primer*. Reaktion, London.

Amidon, J. (2003) *Radical Landscapes – Reinventing Outdoor Space*. Thames & Hudson, London.

Blanc, P. (2008) *Vertical Gardens – From Nature to the City*. Norton, London.

Bradley-Hole, C. (2007) *Making the Modern Garden*. Mitchell-Beazley, London.

Bradley-Hole, C. (1999) *The Minimalist Garden*. Mitchell-Beazley, London.

Cooper, G. & Taylor, G. (2000) *Visions of Paradise* (Fernando Caruncho). Monacelli, New York.

Cooper, P. (2006) *Gardens Without Boundaries*. Mitchell-Beazley, London.

Cooper, P. (2003) *Interiorscapes*. Mitchell-Beazley, London.

Cooper, P. (2001) *Living Sculpture*. Mitchell-Beazley, London.

Cooper, P. (2007) *The New Tech Garden*. Mitchell-Beazley, London.

Hunt, B. & Whateley, E. (2008) *Creative Connections – Aspects of the Garden Design Process*. Packard, Chichester.

Jencks, C. A. (2005) *The Garden of Cosmic Speculation*. Frances Lincoln, London.

Johanson, P. (2006) *Art and Survival*. Islands Institute, New York.

Macgowan, T. (2010) *Transforming Uncommon Ground* (Vladimir Sitta). Frances Lincoln, London.

Oehme, W. & Van Sweden, J. (1990) *Bold Romantic Gardens*. Acropolis, Reston.

Richardson, T. (2008) *Avant Gardeners – Fifty Visionaries of the Contemporary Landscape*. Thames & Hudson, London.

Richardson, T. (2011) *Futurescapes – Designers for Tomorrow's Outdoor Spaces*. Thames & Hudson, London.

Richardson, T., ed. (2004) *The Vanguard Gardens and Landscapes of Martha Schwartz*. Thames & Hudson, London.

Taylor, P., ed. (2011) *The Wirtz Gardens*. Exhibitions International, Leuven.

Tiberghien, G. (1995) *Land Art*. Art Data, London.

Trulove, J. G. (2001) *Ten Landscapes: Topher Delaney*. Rockport, Hove.

Index

Acres Wild 4-5
    private house & garden, Surrey 4-5
Art
    Conceptual 6, 14
    Installation 33
    Kinetic 43
    Land 6
    Performance 8
    Pop 6, 20, 31
autism 94-101
autobiographical interpretation 14, 22, 23, 33, 60, 64

Bacon, Francis 21
Barton, Julia 10, 11
    'Resurrection', Savannah GA 11
BCA Landscape 16, 17
    'Face of Liverpool' 17
Blake, Peter 60
Blanc, Patrick 45-46
    Athenaeum Hotel, London 45
Bradley-Hole, Christopher 1
briefs, client 13, 17, 19, 28, 41
Brookes, John 4
Bulaitis, Bonita 86, 87

Cao, Andy 23-24
    'Glass Garden', Los Angeles 23
Chaumont-sur-Loire, France 8
Chelsea Flower Show gardens, Paul Cooper's 58, 60, 66, 68, 76. 88,
children 42, 78
client
    briefs 13, 17, 19, 41
    histories 17-18
colour 8, 31, 32
compositional methodology 26

conceptualism, conceptualist design vii, viii, 4, 6, 9, 11, 12, 14, 24
    interactive 94-101
    narrative approach 26-29, 56-67
    planting 11, 12, 29, 33, 73, 84-85, 87
    sensory approach 94-101
    theatrical & kinetic effects 32, 41-42, 43, 78-79, 80-81
    visual approach 29-31
Cooper, Paul, designs
    'Allegorical Garden', Gloucestershire 28-29, 56-57
    'A Biographical Odyssey', London 17-18, 64-65
    'A Boy's Own Garden', Chelsea Flower Show 60-61
    'The Climate Cases', Chelsea Flower Show 88-89
    'Cool & Sexy Garden', Chelsea Flower Show 76-77
    'The Eden Laboratory', Métis Garden Festival 90-92
    'A Football Fantasy', London 62-63
    'The Ford 'Carden'', BBC Gardener's World Live Show, Birmingham 82-83
    Garden Room, Leonard Hotel, London 54-55
    'The Greening of Industry', Chelsea Flower Show 58-59
    Grizedale Forest Sculpture Trail, 50
    'Hanging Garden', Chelsea Flower Show 68-69
    'Heavy Metal Garden', Gloucestershire 46, 84-85
    'Instant Garden', BBC TV 'Gardens by Design' 38, 70-73
    'Just What Is It?' Hampton Court Flower Show 39, 74-75
    'Landscape for Measuring Distance & Time', Cumbria 7
    'Multi-media Garden', London 41-42, 78-79
    'Night Garden', London 32, 80-81
    'Ocean to a Garden', Chelsea Flower Show 66-67
    'The Prism Garden', London 87
    Roof Garden, Chelsea, London 51
    'The Rothko Garden', London 86
    'Sensory Garden', Newbus Grange 94-101
    'The Square Dance Garden', Hodgkinson Psychiatric Unit, Lincoln 19, 91
    'Torrens', Weybridge 34-35, 52-53
    'Two Circles in a Stone Bridge', Dorset ii, 48-49
    'Underground Garden', London viii
Cooper, Paul, manifesto 37
Cormier, Claude vii, 9, 10, 18, 31
    Place d'Youville, Montréal 10
    'Lipstick Forest', Montréal 31

Dadaism 6
Delaney, Topher vii, 4, 5, 15, 16, 40
    'Blue Garden', San Francisco 40
    private residence, San Francisco 5
    'Courtyard Garden', University of San Francisco 15, 16
design process 13-46
Duchamp, Marcel 6

ergonomics 9
Ernst, Max 82

Ford Motor Company 82
Fullard, George 60
functional elements 9, 68

garden
    as art 8
    construction 35
    festivals 8, 22 and see Chelsea Flower Shows
    history 27, 30, 62, 66
    innovation 37
    reusable/portable 68, 71
    vertical 45-46, 69
    virtual 32
garden design
    Arts & Crafts 4
    conceptualist 8
    conventional 1, 4, 5
    decorative 4
    minimalist/modernist 1, 4, 52
    naturalistic 4
    post-modernism 4
    zen 4
Gehry, Frank O 43
Gorman, Cliff 38, 70-72
Gormley, Anthony 21

Hall, Janis 6
Hamilton, Richard 39, 74
hard landscape 9
Heizer, Michael 6
Heywood, Tony 22, 33
    'The Calling' 22
    'The Echo' 33
historical references 16, 17, 27, 62, 66
Hockney, David 39, 75
Hunt, Barbara viii, 9
hydroponics 45

'Idea', the vii, 1-3, 4, 6, 9, 10, 11, 12, 13, 24, 29
information gathering 13-14, 17, 22
inspiration 14-24

installations 86, 87
interactive gardens 94-101

Jencks, Charles 6
Johanson, Patricia 21-22
    'Endangered Garden & Ribbon Worm',
      nr San Francisco 21
kinetic devices 43
Kunz, Samm 46

landscape
    hard 9
    soft 10, 12
    zones 12
lateral thinking 18, 27, 31
Lichtenstein, Roy 43, 79
lifestyle 37
light, lighting 32, 42, 79, 80-81
linear methodology 26
Lutsko, Ron 12
    Ranch south of San Francisco 12

materials 9, 10, 20, 22, 23, 24, 27, 34-40, 48,
    66, 70-72, 87, 88, 93, 94-101
methodology 26
Métis, Québec 8, 90-92
Mitani, Toru 43-44
    YKK Research & Development Centre,
      Tokyo 43-44
Montréal 9, 10
Moore, Henry 21
motifs,
    traditional viii
    visual 18, 19-21

narrative approach, design 26-29
Nash, Paul 1, 3
Newbus Grange, Darlington 94-101
Nicholson, Ben 35, 53

Oehme, Wolfgang 10
Oldenburg, Claus 31

packaging, product 21
paths 9
pattern 29
Performance Art 8
Place d'Youville, Montréal 9, 10
Plant Architect Inc. 24-25
    Sweet Farm, Québec 24, 25
plants, plant material 8, 10, 11, 42, 45, 85, 86,
    87, 88, 91-92, 97-98
Pommer, Christopher 25
Pop Art 6, 20, 21, 31
Pope, Alexander 15

Rapoport, Lisa 25
references
    historical 16
    visual 15
repetition in design 29, 30
restraint, design strategy 25-26
Richardson, Tim vii, 4, 6, 12, 20
Rothko, Mark 86

San Francisco CA 5, 12, 16, 21, 40
Schlemmer, Oskar 96
Schwartz, Martha vii, 18, 20, 26-27, 29-30
    'Splice Garden', Cambridge, MA 26-27
sculpture 6
sensory gardens 94-101
shock 74, 76
site-specific design ii, 14, 26, 29
sites,
    activities, purpose 15
    'as found' 25
    conditions 9, 10, 15, 24, 26, 32, 42
    history 13, 16
    information gathering 13-14

Sitta, Vladimir 21, 29
Smith, Ken 14
Smithson, Robert 6
sound systems 51
source material 14
storyboards 28
strategies, design 13, 14, 15-26
    project-specific 18
    site-based 15, 24, 25, 26
style 10, 22
    personal *see* autobiographical
      interpretation

theatrical effects 32, 41-42, 43, 78-79
Thomson, Andy 16
Toll, Julie 1
Topotek 1 18

van der Rohe, Mies 4
Van Sweden, James 10
virtual gardens 32
visual references 15, 20, 29

Wagner, Keith 25-26
    'Hilltop' Residence, Vermont 25-26
Ward, Nathaniel Bagshaw 88
West 8, urban & landscape architects 29, 34, 35
    'Interpolis' Garden, Tilburg 35
Whateley, Elizabeth viii, 9
Whitehead Institute, Cambridge, MA 26, 27
Wirtz, Jacques 10

XP Gar magazine 77